"Too many of us in America have lost our way. John Bryant gives you hope. All you've got to do is read, listen, act. Every one of us can do it. You can do it!"
—Peter Georgescu, Chairman Emeritus, Young & Rubicam

"John Hope Bryant is a beacon of light for the economically disaffected. If ever there was a one-stop shop for 21st-century life and career advice, this is it."
—Clare Woodcraft-Scott, CEO, Emirates Foundation

"This book gives us the necessary vision and real-life practical tools to climb our financial mountain and enjoy the beautiful sunny summit that we deserve."
—Özlem Denizmen, entrepreneur, Young Global Leader, author, and spearhead of the financial literacy movement in Turkey

"This book delivers the missing ingredient in the financial lives of too many people today: hope."
—Chris Gardner, owner and CEO, Christopher Gardner International Holdings

"John is giving his readers raw examples of his personal life in hopes of empowering them to invest in themselves, to be responsible, and to make the world a better place for all of us."
—Rev. Dr. C. T. Vivian, founder of C. T. Vivian Leadership Institute

"John's call for people to aspire to build something has the power to transform America and the rest of the world at a time when technological breakthroughs are making millions more jobs obsolete."
—Karim Hajji, CEO, Casablanca Stock Exchange

"John Hope Bryant has once again written an essential book. *The Memo* is nothing less than a field manual for success in the 21st century."
—Paul Smyke, Head of North America and Member of the Executive Committee, World Economic Forum, LLC

"*The Memo* is a fresh and inspirational take on how to think about money, success, and personal fulfillment."
—Ellen Alemany, Chairwoman and CEO, CIT Group

"This book will ensure that wealth is developed not only in financial capital but also through the mental capacity that makes it timeless."
—Phuti Mahanyele, Executive Chairperson, Sigma Capital

"At a time when so many believe that the American Dream is dead, *The Memo* offers hope in the form of a prescription for prosperity."
—Frank Martell, President and CEO, CoreLogic, Inc.

The
MEMO

**FIVE RULES
FOR YOUR
ECONOMIC
LIBERATION**

The
MEMO

JOHN HOPE BRYANT

BK

Berrett–Koehler Publishers, Inc.
a BK Life book

Berrett-Koehler Publishers, Inc.
1333 Broadway, Suite 1000
Oakland, CA 94612-1921
Tel: (510) 817-2277 | Fax: (510) 817-2278 | www.bkconnection.com

ORDERING INFORMATION
Quantity sales. Special discounts are available on quantity purchases by corporations, associations, and others. For details, contact the "Special Sales Department" at the Berrett-Koehler address above.
Individual sales. Berrett-Koehler publications are available through most bookstores. They can also be ordered directly from Berrett-Koehler: Tel: (800) 929-2929; Fax: (802) 864-7626; www.bkconnection.com.
Orders for college textbook/course adoption use. Please contact Berrett-Koehler: Tel: (800) 929-2929; Fax: (802) 864-7626.
Orders by U.S. trade bookstores and wholesalers. Please contact Ingram Publisher Services: Tel: (800) 509-4887; Fax: (800) 838-1149; E-mail: customer.service@ingrampublisherservices.com; or visit www.ingrampublisherservices.com/Ordering for details about electronic ordering.

Berrett-Koehler and the BK logo are registered trademarks of Berrett-Koehler Publishers, Inc.

Printed in the United States of America

Berrett-Koehler books are printed on long-lasting acid-free paper. When it is available, we choose paper that has been manufactured by environmentally responsible processes. These may include using trees grown in sustainable forests, incorporating recycled paper, minimizing chlorine in bleaching, or recycling the energy produced at the paper mill.

Library of Congress Cataloging-in-Publication Data
NAMES: Bryant, John, 1966–   author.
TITLE: The memo : five rules for your economic liberation / by John Hope Bryant.
DESCRIPTION: First edition. | Oakland, CA : Berrett-Koehler Publishers, Inc., [2017]
IDENTIFIERS: LCCN 2017019207 | ISBN 9781523084562 (hardcover)
SUBJECTS: LCSH: Financial literacy. | Wealth. | Social mobility. | Entrepreneurship.
CLASSIFICATION: LCC HG179 .B7933 2017 | DDC 332.024/01—dc23
LC record available at https://lccn.loc.gov/2017019207

First Edition
22 21 20 19 18 17 | 10 9 8 7 6 5 4 3 2 1

Book producer and text designer: BookMatters, Berkeley, CA
Copyeditor: Mike Mollett
Proofreader: Janet Reed Blake
Indexer: Leonard Rosenbaum
Cover designer: Dan Tesser, Studio Carnelian

To the Invisible Class—the struggling, the unseen, the ones who didn't get the Memo.

CONTENTS

FOREWORD

If every young person did everything John Hope Bryant recommends in this book, America and the world would change. Human development would boom. We would see millions of new jobs, high well-being and, yes, fabulous credit scores coast to coast. We would all have more freedom.

What John recommends in this book is simple and doable. His solutions to many of America's problems don't cost anything. Actually, the solutions for you, me, and our cities and counties are free.

And we're not being asked to do the impossible. John is challenging us simply to be our best selves. And he is telling us exactly how to do it.

He tells us to live within our means because financial responsibility creates freedom. John tells us to get up and work hard because there are no limits when our hope is high. He tells us to own a home. He tells us to keep our promises.

What he speaks of most of all is *building*. He says we need to become "a Nation of Builders."

John himself is a builder. He built Operation HOPE, which teaches financial literacy and has changed millions of lives. He himself has a very successful life and has become a famous, important American because he built something. In this book, he challenges us to build something.

During our young lives, our family, teachers, and friends ask us, "What do you want to do when you grow up?" or "What kind of job do you want to have?"

Literally no one ever asks us, "What do you want to build?"

What if we all read this book and then changed how we develop people? Rather than asking them, "Where will you work?" we would ask them, "What can you build?"

Dream and build anything. It could be a small- or medium-sized business. Or a huge business—one of $10 million or $10 billion in sales. They all count and add up to the sum total of America and the world. We need hundreds of thousands of small- and medium-sized businesses—any society needs them continuously starting up and shooting up—or our society can't develop.

Young people can also build a small, medium, or large nonprofit. Nonprofits create economic energy, too. They boost gross domestic product (GDP) and create real jobs and real city and state growth. So do megachurches, a new children's museum, a chain of day care centers, or home health nonprofits. Or charities to assist disadvantaged citizens.

All of these organizations or institutions require a business model and a gifted builder, or they never take off. They literally never create new economic energy in the absence of a born builder.

At some point in John's life, he decided to build a big nonprofit to make America and the world a better place. John gets up every day and builds. He tells us that entrepreneurship is the great American way and the only thing that will save America and our almighty middle class.

The greatest point of all is that you and I and the whole country must create a new future for America and the world. But that it must be done from the bottom up rather than the top down. I think that is the most profound thought I have heard in twenty years.

John is right, and this book is right.

Jim Clifton, Chairman and CEO of Gallup,
author of The Coming Jobs War

PREFACE

History has shown that when societies fall apart, they fray first from the bottom, and then the top falls inward. So it is an article of common sense to me that we all need to work hard to strengthen the so-called bottom of our society. Particularly because this is the group that has always made up the true strivers of society.

The bottom is where society's builders come from every hundred years or so. We must once again become a Nation of Builders.

We must continue to work to revitalize hope and a sense of opportunity for the people at the bottom—the people for whom the system is not currently working—to create a pathway forward. Expanding opportunity, providing a level playing field where the rules are published and there exists fair play for all, and ultimately providing the tools and essential services for the true empowerment of the person—these are the aims of Operation HOPE.

Providing dignity for all. Building an economy for all. These and more are the building blocks of hope.

We live today in strained and trying times, from racial tensions and poverty in the United States, to immigrant tensions and poverty in Europe, to military tensions and poverty in the Middle East, to abusive tensions and poverty in Latin America, to authoritarian tensions and poverty throughout large parts of Asia and the African continent. And then you have a toxic mix of these things in many truly troubled parts of the world. But consistent among all the regions of the world is the challenge of *poverty*.

The poverty I speak of is different than the poverty you were taught about in school or you hear about in the news. The poverty you were taught about is what I call "sustenance poverty," a numerical understanding of at what level the available food, shelter, and health care is simply not enough. Beyond solving for the critically important human dignity areas of hunger, shelter, and other basic life necessities, the sort of poverty I speak of here is the most devastating to the human spirit.

This poverty, which I first outlined in the HOPE Doctrine on Poverty in *How the Poor Can Save Capitalism*, is first and foremost one of lost confidence and devastated esteem (the first 50 percent).

Bad role models and a negative, repressive environment follow (the next 25 percent).

The final 25 percent consists of a lack of aspiration, which is a code word for hope, and no clear path to mainstream opportunity.

The most dangerous person in the world is a person with no hope.

A poverty of the soul and spirit perverts the good direction of a person, leading to a whole host of bad things, including depression and lost hope. This type of poverty is dangerous to the very fabric of a sustainable global society. It is the one thing that works against our own well-being in the world the most.

I formed Operation HOPE to combat poverty in all its guises and forms.

The HOPE Doctrine on Wealth

This book is my view of the world—its problems and its possibilities—through an economic lens. As I unpack the book, I will refer to the commonly used word *capital* in a different way. The word *capital* comes from the Latin root word *capita* or "knowledge in the head." In other words, capital at its core has nothing to do with money. And, by the way, neither does true, sustainable wealth.

If I give a homeless man a million dollars, he will be broke in six months. If I observe a rich man with no "knowledge in the head," I will find him broke within a generation or less. As an early English proverb states, "A fool and his money are soon parted."

And so, in this book, I present a new HOPE Doctrine on Wealth, outlined below and discussed at length later in the book.

True wealth has little to do with money. My own wealth, as an example, came from my embrace of the free-enterprise system, my opportunity mind-set, my critically important relationship capital, my entrepreneurial hustle, and finally my unwavering belief in myself—my spiritual capital. I unpack all of this in the book.

You will find that the wealthy in the world possess confidence and self-esteem (the first 50 percent of true wealth).

Either through their natural family or people they've met along the way, they all also have good role models and an enabling environment (the next 25 percent).

Finally, they have high aspirations (hope), and they all generally see opportunity everywhere (the last 25 percent).

Together, these make up a formula for a new and achievable HOPE Doctrine on Wealth.

But how do people get there?

What are the building blocks and the steps forward when almost none of these enabling factors are present in your life?

What is the magic sauce that the wealthy and successful have that the struggling classes somehow missed out on?

Certainly, it is not because one group is better than the other. Because they are not. I have seen brilliant men and women who are homeless, and I have seen idiots and fools with money.

The missing sauce is the Memo.

What Is the Memo and Who Didn't Get It?

A super majority of people here in the United States and around the world have one thing in common: They never got what I call "the Memo." They were never told how this world actually works.

How do you prosper? How do you excel? At a more defensive and basic level, how do you protect yourself from societal injustices and a lack of fair play in the twenty-first century?

These are questions I address directly in this book (it's less of a "how-to" and more of a "how-to-think").

While I've placed the full version of the Memo at the beginning of the book, everything you really need to know can be summed up in just a couple of sentences:

> **Your power comes from economic independence, which is also what protects you against social injustice, economic manipulation, and profiling on all levels. Nobody is going to give you that power. You must gain it for yourself. Don't waste time on anger; instead, use your inner capital to level the playing field.**

This super majority of people who never got the Memo make up what I call the Invisible Class. They come in all shapes, colors, and sizes.

The Invisible Class includes American urban youth with too much time on their hands. Even when they have a real passion for success and a desire for economic freedom, they don't have enough education to differentiate themselves in a market economy. Worst of all, they don't possess enough real opportunity in their lives to divert their attention from the dangerous and life-altering call of the streets.

It includes rural adults in small towns with a high school education, good hands, and a hearty work ethic that fifty years ago would have earned them a "family wage" with blue-collar skills. But these "assets" provide not much of any real aspirational value today.

They are residents of the poor and disconnected suburbs in cities throughout Europe. I am talking about people in the areas right outside of Paris and London who have rioted in recent years against the changes they see happening to their way of living.

I am talking about large swaths of people under the age

of twenty-five in the Middle East and North Africa region—increasingly, the majority of the populations in countries such as Saudi Arabia and Morocco. Young, educated, Internet-connected, jobless, and frustrated.

The Invisible Class is the immigrants flooding into countries from civil war–ravaged lands the world over.

The Invisible Class includes gang members and gang organizers. They are the illegal, unethical entrepreneurs that the world knows to be drug dealers. Dumb (in terms of their business plans and chosen toxic professions), but far from stupid.

Some members of the Invisible Class join ISIS because they don't fit in anywhere else and resent what feels like the unfairness of the world.

The Invisible Class also includes the struggling American middle class, people making an average of $50,000 a year and still having "too much month at the end of their money."

The Invisible Class is people who are outside of the economic system of success, and they don't really know why, so understandably they get frustrated by it. They are angry with it. They don't know how to get ahead in the midst of the growing global competition for jobs and opportunity.

In the United States, for example, these are people who are not truly "seen" by the economy, by politicians, by public policy makers, by big business interests, or even largely by academics and the media. Worst of all, increasingly, they don't even see themselves. They don't see their own potential. They—like the aspirational nation they live in—have lost what I call their "storyline." They have lost connection with that special sauce in America that made this nation successful in the first place. They have totally disconnected from the fact that most of the wealth in this nation and in almost every other developed country in the world (with the exception of wealth through government contracting or crime) came from poor people.

The Invisible Class is people who are experiencing a twenty-first-century crisis of confidence and personal faith, which is impacting their self-esteem.

People in this group are giving in to fear and giving up hope that they can realize their dreams. They don't even think that their children will do better than they have. Truth be told, they are pretty confident that their children will do worse.

People in the Invisible Class don't feel seen, and, this I know for sure, everyone wants to be seen. Everyone wants to know that they count. They want to know that they matter and that what they believe, do, and think is important.

This group equals more than 150 million people in the United States of America, and more than five billion of the world's seven billion population around the world.

These are people—black, white, brown, red, or yellow—who never got the Memo.

The people in this group have a lot in common (despite racial differences), but they have been pitted against each other.

"Someone (other than me) has to be the one to blame for the mess called my life," goes the narrative, which plays on deep fears of a class environment and standards of living in constant decline.

This narrative is offensive to the soul, as it gets each subgroup further and further from the essential truths about their respective lives, truths needed for a reawakening of their potential.

Who Is This Book For?

In writing this book, my demographic changed. It expanded.

I wrote this book because it sticks in my brain that the wealthiest eighty-five individuals have more wealth than 3.5 billion people on the planet, and this is simply not sustainable. It is immoral. It is not good—even for the wealthy that belong to the club of eighty-five.

Even more troubling to me, in the United States, the wealthiest 1 percent captured 95 percent of the post–financial crisis growth since 2009, while the bottom 90 percent became poorer.

This book is for the bottom 90 percent.

It is not just for people with low credit scores in rundown neighborhoods. It is for everyone who is struggling. I am speaking to black and white, rich and poor, Republican and Democrat, anyone who is seeing their life seep away—and wants their dream back.

This book is for you no matter where you are. You may have gotten one or two of the five rules of economic independence, but you still don't *feel* economically independent. You may have a 725 credit score, but you're sitting at your computer all day and your relationships are dwindling, and you're unable to get ahead. You may be sitting there thinking, "If I'm doing all the right things and still struggling, then the system has to be rigged."

No, actually, there's just some important stuff nobody told you. Nobody gave you the Memo.

I wrote this book for you.

In looking forward toward solutions for us all, I don't normally address issues of race and division. But in this instance I believe that I must speak to them, as they are tied to both our history and our shared future. I need to address them before we can move forward.

This book is for everyone, certainly for the majority of people in the world of every race living from paycheck to paycheck— everyone with too much month at the end of their money, including the struggling middle class. But I also speak directly here to Black America because I am convinced that more than any other race we have been almost violently harmed by not getting the original Memo.

This was not the way it was supposed to happen after the Emancipation Proclamation. The first Memo for black Americans dates back to 1865 and President Lincoln's vision for a "freed man's bank" with the radical mission to teach freed slaves about money, to introduce them to the free-enterprise system.

Lincoln and Frederick Douglass knew that true freedom for freed slaves relied on self-determination and that you cannot "self-determine" in the modern world without understanding business and capitalism. Or to quote civil rights leader, and my mentor, Andrew Young, "To live in a system of free enterprise and to not understand free enterprise must be the very definition of slavery."

The partnership between Lincoln and Douglass was sidetracked due to Lincoln's assassination, so I have decided to pick their work up today, that is, to teach the basic rules of capital and economic independence to those who most need to know them.

It is easy to get angry and frustrated. And there are good reasons, too. But none of that will help you. None of that will give you economic power.

Instead, turn your anger into positive energy.

Consider a suit maker who didn't know he could ever be a business owner by the name of Ryan Taylor. He was an early client of Operation HOPE, and I first wrote about him in *How the Poor Can Save Capitalism.*

Ryan came to me as a young man with the dream of working for a New York fashion house, but I had to tell him straight out that he would probably never be hired by any of them. It so happens that he is African American, but you could also say that he didn't have the right relationship capital to be seen. He was a member of the Invisible Class.

No one knew him in the fashion world, which is a closed loop of relationships like no other. They hook up their friends and their friends' friends, the people they know and who look like them. I told him not to get mad about this, that this was the way of the world.

I told him he should focus on writing checks, not cashing them. Become the owner of a fashion house of his own versus trying to work for someone else who didn't really want him.

Ryan took the time to secure his knowledge and understanding of how money and the free-enterprise system worked. He raised his credit score over several months so we could get him approved for a small bank loan for his scheduled start-up capital. He built up his inner confidence and his belief in himself and his abilities.

He stepped out of the Invisible Class forever and began to

win. He got the Memo, and today I buy my business suits from Ryan Taylor.

This book forces you to look at some of the most controversial aspects of life through an economic lens and from a nonemotional perspective, just like Ryan did.

And now it's time to unpack the game, to unpack real power, and then to repack it—with a focus on the Invisible Class. I guarantee you, the game is not what you think.

Let's learn to win it.

The
MEMO

True power in this world comes from economic independence; this is also your primary protection from social injustice, political manipulation, and profiling.

Nobody can give you economic independence— you must gain it for yourself.

You, and only you, can gain this power from the way that you manage your "inner capital." This inner capital is made up of your mind-set, relationships, knowledge, and spirit. Financial capital (money or wealth) is a function of how you invest your inner capital.

If you have inner capital, you can never be truly poor. If you lack inner capital, all the money in the world cannot set you free. Once you have satisfied your basic sustenance needs—food, water, health, and a roof over your head—poverty has more to do with your head than your wallet.

The
FIVE SIMPLE RULES for ECONOMIC INDEPENDENCE

1. We Live in a Free-Enterprise System—
    Embrace It.

2. Your Mind-Set Makes or Loses Money
    and Wealth—You Choose.

3. Your Relationships Are Investments—
    Build Relationship Capital with Yourself First.

4. Don't Just Get a Job—Be Entrepreneurial.

5. Spiritual Capital Is the Start of True Wealth—
    Own Your Power.

GETTING THE MEMO

On April 7, 2016, I did what I thought would be a fairly routine radio interview with commentator and friend Roland Martin. The topic was turning our inner city and our underserved communities around, and I assumed it would be a straightforward discussion. No drama here, I thought.

I was dead wrong.

During the course of the interview, I mentioned something I wrongly assumed everyone already knew: Slavery was first and foremost economic in nature. It was about money and wealth before it was about anything else. It was about free labor.

The radio station switchboard lit up.

I went on to explain that slavery—as immoral and cruel as it obviously was—was primarily and at its core about building a country for free, and building wealth for some (i.e., Southern plantation owners) through what I call "bad capitalism."

The message board on the *Roland Martin Show* was going crazy, and not in a good way. But I hadn't a clue; I just kept on talking.

To me, this was plain common sense. It was not an emotional issue for me. It was simply a stack of statistical facts for us all to understand and a problem for us to then solve: how do we go forward?

It wasn't that I didn't feel the injustice. I did and I do. My great-great-grandfather on my father's side was born on a Southern plantation in the Deep South. Mississippi, to be exact.

My grandmother on my mother's side gave birth to her children in a shotgun shack in Alabama, later moving the entire family to the relative luxury of East St. Louis (for those who don't know East St. Louis, "relative luxury" is a joke).

Yes, I do understand the injustice. I *do* feel the pain.

But I also know that my feelings and my emotions about it do nothing to help right this wrong or to help move us forward from the effects of that period, many of which linger on even to this day.

I knew that I would need my brain for that task. I needed to be clearheaded and nonemotional, too. I needed to work from the neck up.

My listening audience on this day saw things through a completely different lens, though. They were pissed. At me.

I went on to explain during the course of the interview that in 2016, we still have a version of what I call modern slavery in our own urban, inner-city neighborhoods, and this so-called enslavement is all economic.

In these places, fully 99 percent of all our most pressing challenges and daily stresses—from joblessness to crime and violent crime, to high homicide rates, to high school dropout rates, to massive levels of the most basic illiteracy, crushed family structures, and an overwhelming lack of homeownership and business ownership—were focused in 500-credit-score neighborhoods.

You can literally take a 500-credit-score map and overlay it on top of all the worst problems plaguing all the communities in which people in our Invisible Class reside—urban, suburban, and rural. They match up perfectly.

But for me it's not really about the credit score; it's about identifying powerful and yet unseen trend lines and intersection points that are or could be transformational for communities. Credit scores are leading indicators, trend lines for the kind of energy present in a neighborhood.

To me, credit scores—very much *unlike* racism or bias or discrimination and countless other things that bedevil the Invisible Class (and the African American race of people specifically) on a daily basis—are fantastic because they are so measureable.

They are just one powerful example of a nonemotional scientific indicator of success that lets you feel good about the progress you are making. You can see how the changes you are making move your score up the chart—and believe me, a 100-point increase in your credit score signals an improvement in your life around much more than just your score! It signals more options, more freedom, more hope.

But while I was busy being rational and nonemotional on the topic, large portions of the listening audience were going stark raving mad, lashing out at me wherever they could track me down on social media.

I discovered this mini-crisis of confidence (in me) within my own community on my way to the airport in Washington,

DC. It was bad, and it was constant. I simply couldn't keep up with the barrage of criticism, complete with folks calling me an Uncle Tom and a coon, in a continual stream of inter-changeable phrases. I was being bullied and overwhelmed on social media, mostly on my Twitter account.

Luckily, I was able to set this critiquing of me aside and to think clearly—once again from the neck up—about what was really going on here and what was really important. And I quickly found that 140 characters on Twitter was simply insuf-ficient to communicate what I really meant.

What We Don't Know That We Don't Know

I remember having some powerful thoughts about what I was hearing and experiencing from my people on that day:

1. We are emotional in response to our problems.

2. We are frustrated in relation to our lack of being seen or heard.

3. We are all too often simply "angry for a living."

4. Worst of all, we are becoming cynical as a new and constant norm.

I remembered that powerful Malcolm X quote in which he laments, "You've been took. You've been hoodwinked. Bam-boozled. . . ."

It is precisely what I thought was happening at the time. But this time, it was *us* tricking *ourselves*.

We could not hear, yet alone analyze, a clearheaded and wide-eyed presentation of the facts because our emotions had taken over. And when that happens, the racist that everyone despises and says they are rallying against actually wins. When our emotions distract us from the real truths, then our hope dies. And the one thing I know for sure from my twenty-five years with Operation HOPE is that the most dangerous person in the world is a person with no hope.

I decided that I had to do something.

I believed that there were a whole set of facts, realities— even opportunities—that we were missing altogether, because we were so utterly focused on our pain. We felt that this pain made us invisible, unheard, and unimportant, and we were determined to have our pain noticed.

Understandable? Yes. But productive? No.

I believe that membership in the Invisible Class today—and certainly our ability to leave the Invisible Class tomorrow— has less to do with our history and more to do with our credit scores (and what we do to raise them).

I believe that getting the Memo triggers very real and sustainable resolutions to a vast majority of problems plaguing my community and other communities of poor, struggling, and powerless people the world over (i.e., the Invisible Class)— including my poor white brothers and sisters right here in rural America.

I wanted to share that message with my dissenters. But first I needed to regain the higher ground—and get a little personal dignity back, too.

I could not be a punk and simply retreat behind the safe walls of my comfortable home and my curated private life.

I could not simply return to my successful business because I did not like the response that my people offered me.

I needed to step up, because while I was convinced that my people were utterly brilliant, in this case, it was what we didn't know that we didn't know (but that we thought we knew!) that was killing us. And so, I responded, writ large.

I took to a tool I had just discovered (also through Roland Martin) called Facebook Live.

I recorded a short eight-minute video en route to the airport entitled "Modern Slavery," and I did it live so I could not punk out later and not publish.

I recorded a passionate and powerful message, stepped out of the car and right into the airport terminal, preparing myself for the avalanche of what I assumed would be even more ramped-up criticisms.

The central message of the video was this:

> While we are busy being angry, exhausting ourselves chasing a racism and bias ghost that is akin to the boogeyman of our childhood, in urban, inner-city, and rural underserved neighborhoods something else very real and tangible is happening—and you can actually see and do something about it!
>
> In each and every one of those communities, here is what you see: a check casher, next to a payday loan lender, next to a rent-to-own-store, next to a renting rims store (yes, I mean twenty-inch rims for your car with spinners attached), next to a liquor store.
>
> What does this mean? It means a one-trillion-dollar junk credit industry is not only preying on you, they are effectively robbing you and those you love in plain sight. In broad daylight.
>
> And they are not even preying on black communities per se. They are targeting the 500-credit-score customer,

regardless of race. Literally targeting them. I promise you'll see every color of the rainbow in the faces of people standing in line for a payday loan.

If you live in rural poor white America, you see the same check-cashing stores, the same crumbling storefronts, the same low-quality food options as you do in poor urban neighborhoods. If you live on a military base, which includes all races of people, you will see much the same, plus other businesses that signal despair and depression.

Heck, given our low level of financial literacy and understanding of money and the market economy, you are now beginning to see these same things in working middle-class neighborhoods that also never got the Memo.

And so today these groups feel just as ignored and invisible as the black youth in our inner cities. Everyone wants to feel seen.

My point was that the base of all our problems is economic in nature. But all too often, far too many of us see the economic status quo as normal.

It is not normal.

And the result of my bold retort? More than three million video views, eleven thousand comments, and twenty thousand shares on this short eight-minute video—and 95 percent of the comments were positive, supportive, and affirming.

Even better, it was the overwhelmingly African American audience of commenters that began the pushback against the coon and Uncle Tom criticisms directed at me. They explained to the others not only what I really meant but also how they were 100 percent with it—and with me.

So, What Are We Going to Do About It?

The majority of commenters who responded positively to my video understood that racism is like rain: It's either falling someplace or it's gathering someplace else. You might as well get out an umbrella and start strolling through it—it's not going to change, and so we must.

It was then that I knew we had a chance for a new movement, a movement to liberate the Invisible Class from predators and indifference, to change (i.e., empower) ourselves because we cannot always change the ignorance and backwardness of others around us.

Essentially, the Memo says this: I know and recognize that we are dealing with serious problems of inequality and unfairness. AND NOW WHAT? What are we going to do about it?

What we do is we change our narrative by living well. That is what this book is about. *The Memo* gives you five simple rules for moving forward to economic independence. I promise these rules apply to you wherever you are, whoever you are.

Let's go.

We Live in a Free-Enterprise System— Embrace It

Money runs the world from the moment you wake up until the moment you hit your pillow and head to sleep. Actually, money is even intersecting every aspect of your life while you sleep!

I am talking about YOUR life, not some random person you don't know and cannot relate to. I am not talking about a city's economics, or a company's balance sheet or revenue, or a country's identity, brand, or GDP. I am talking about YOU.

So, you doubt me? Okay, that's understandable. Check this out:

You woke up this morning at 6 a.m., 7 a.m., 8 a.m., or whatever. What precisely woke you up? An alarm clock, or an alarm setting on your mobile phone or smartphone? That's money, folks. (It's actually more than that. It's entrepreneurship, which I address in Rule 4 in the book.) You or someone who loves you spent hard-fought-for cash money for that alarm clock or phone. No one got it for free.

You pulled back the sheets someone purchased and rolled out of the bed that someone purchased and put your feet on the ground of a house or an apartment that someone is paying for (even in most public housing the tenants pay a portion of the rent out of their own pockets).

You put on the slippers you or someone paid for, and walked into your bathroom to brush your teeth—with toothpaste and a toothbrush that someone paid for.

You washed up with soap and dried yourself with towels that someone paid for.

You then walked to the refrigerator that someone bought, and nourished yourself with food that someone purchased, probably that same week.

As you walked out the door, you turned off the lights and other utilities that you or someone else is paying the bill for.

You plopped yourself into a car that you pay for, probably on a monthly basis.

You started the car up, and within fifteen minutes you glanced at the gas gauge. If it was low, you pulled into a gas station, and you paid for that gas in real time.

You dropped your children off at day care on the way to work, and while the ladies there are super nice and kind, for sure they are not keeping your crazed-with-energy kids just for the hell of it. You are paying these hardworking people to put up with them. (Smile. I am sure your kids are just angels.)

Late for work after dropping your kids off at day care, you got pulled over for driving too fast on the street, or maybe you got a ticket on the freeway for driving in the carpool lane because it was only you and the blow-up dummy in the car that morning.

The police officer, who could not have been more polite in this instance, did not want an excuse. He did not want an apology. He did not want to hear your sob story or promises for redemption. He wanted your money for your city's coffers, and so he wrote you a ticket. And you didn't get mad, you just paid it—unless of course the radar was lying (smile).

You stressed yourself out to get to work before starting time—let's say 8:30 a.m.—not because you absolutely love punctuality but because you value your job. A job that hopefully you love, or at least enjoy and find fulfilling, but let's face it: It is a job that provides you with a paycheck. You are getting paid to be there, which is at least part of the reason you are there.

And even if you did love your job and would be willing to do it for free if you could afford to do so, you probably wouldn't break your hypothetical neck to get there before 8:30 every morning.

Given a choice and complete economic freedom, you would probably stroll in at whatever time you liked to that job. And this is precisely why my lovely retired mother, who worked hard her entire life to raise her children, build her own nest egg, and take care of her responsibilities, now has a business card that lists her full name—and nothing else.

My mother has no interest whatsoever in being reached by anyone whom she does not fancy now that she can afford to fancy whomever she chooses. Money got my mother to work on time every day for thirty-plus years, and money allows my mother to get up at any time she likes now. She has an 850 credit score, by the way.

So, your being there at work on time every morning (at least I hope this is the case) is all about money. Your money! And there's also this: someone values you enough to pay *you* to be there.

Is the light bulb going on yet for you?

As my best friend, Rod McGrew, once told me, "Even the parking meter that you stopped your car in front of on your way home to pick up some food for dinner has figured out capitalism."

All it does is sit there every day, collecting consistent and impressive passive income from you and everyone else who wants to sit before it on an hourly basis. Every day.

And don't get mad at the parking meter, either. The income it generates allows the city you live in to collect enough money to pay for public services for you and your city.

Take my friend, St. Louis Treasurer Tishaura Jones, who used parking meter fee income to fund financial education for the residents of her city. She even partnered with Operation HOPE and five local banks in town (that benefit from city deposits in their bank vaults) to form and launch the first-ever HOPE Inside location at St. Louis City Hall, where it proudly operates to this very day. All of this was done at no direct cost to city residents, thanks to Tishaura's brilliant thinking. (And by the way, the financial literacy, homeownership, small business, and entrepreneurship classes are all FULL. I just love this, and you should too.)

And now back to an average day in the life of YOU:

You head home after grabbing dinner, which was also paid for with someone's cash, and you and the family sit down at the dinner table, using plates, utensils, even napkins and paper towels that you or someone who loves you paid for. After dinner, maybe you sit down to watch the big-screen television that someone definitely paid for.

And so on, and so on, and so on.

This routine continues until you go to bed with the things and services that occupy every aspect and moment of your life involving money. Even when you are sound asleep, (your) money is at work.

And then, like magic, the entire routine begins again. When you wake up six to eight hours later, it all repeats itself. Just like Groundhog Day.

But most of us never notice any of this. We go through the motions, never noticing the elephant in the living room of our lives. Money.

But where did all of this start? We were born brilliant, correct? So how did we take a turn so wrong—not only down the wrong street but on the wrong expressway, heading in the wrong direction, to the wrong city.

The answer is: we never got the Memo.

Here I Go Again: Why I Love Credit Scores

If you never got the Memo and are a card-carrying member of the Invisible Class, I can predict some basic things about your economic situation. First, your personal finances aren't together—maybe a few of the bills on your kitchen table have red "past due" stamps on them. More importantly, you don't know (or want to know) your credit score. Second, your family finances probably aren't overflowing with hope. You don't own, you rent, and you're not putting away money for your kids' educations. And, in all likelihood, your business plans are nonexistent. You don't see yourself ever running a business, and you couldn't get a business loan even if you'd just invented the best thing since the Ginsu knife.

In short, you are going in the wrong direction down at least one of the three basic paths to financial independence.

Let's start at the beginning. The beginnings of financial literacy come from understanding how our purchases and debts contribute to an invisible (for the Invisible Class) number that determines our economic destiny: the credit score.

A large and growing portion of employers (more than 40 percent at the time of this writing) require a credit check before they will hire you. That means that no matter how smart or qualified you may be—or how brilliant your now-college-educated-child may in fact be—if your or their credit reports stink, you can pretty much forget about getting hired.

But there is hope. This is a challenge that you can do something about. Take one of our clients at HOPE Inside Ebenezer (Dr. Martin Luther King Jr.'s home church in Atlanta), Ms. Eboni Brown.

Here is Eboni's story in her own words:

> I applied to participate in the 700 Credit Score Community after having been denied my dream job. The reason behind that denial was my credit score. It was too low, and I had too many items in collection.
>
> Doubtful that I would get accepted (because my score was so far from 700), I was overwhelmed with joy and so excited when I received the email saying that I had been accepted into the program. This was the opportunity I needed to receive guidance and motivation as well as a game plan to

get my overwhelming debt and falling credit score under control.

After attending the first session, I was elated to see that I was not the only person having debt issues, and that I would be in a cohort of like-minded individuals ready to get their finances in order.

During my tenure in the 700 Credit Score Community, I learned several things. The first, and I believe most important, was that you can't change your credit score overnight. It takes time and patience and the practice of one day at a time.

I learned also to evaluate my lifestyle. I needed to determine the root of the problem. Was I living a caviar and champagne life with a Wendy's and Coca-Cola budget? Was it the mistakes I made in my young adult life that were now catching up to me? Did I just not make enough money?

In all honesty, it was a combination of all of the above. So, based on the principles I learned in the class, I began to budget my money and live within my means. I put aside the thought that I would never become debt-free and have a great score and filled my mind with more positive thoughts.

After adjusting to my new lifestyle and mind-set, I was very anxious to report to my coach all the things that I had put into place and to receive her feedback. During that session, I learned that the work I had done within a three-month time frame had increased my score 52 points. To date, I have increased my score 78 points.

I continue to apply the concepts I learned from the program, and I look forward to learning more. I am excited to cross the finish line and attain a 700-plus credit score. All things are possible!

A credit check is not necessarily a character check, but it amounts to the same thing in this world we live in today.

Eboni chose not to argue with reality but rather to change it. She decided to win.

If you want to start a new business or buy a home, the financing you seek will most likely pivot heavily off your personal credit history. I know this firsthand.

As an entrepreneur with 1,001 ideas coming up in my teenage years, I used to have credit that stunk. I'm talking 500-credit-score range. When I was eighteen years old, I was homeless for six months in Los Angeles, California. Things got so bad and the stress and the harassing calls from creditors so intense that I even considered filing for personal bankruptcy. I'm glad I didn't, but nothing was easy during this period.

I remember signing an auto finance contract to pay more than 18 percent interest to buy a car during that period. I pay 1.99 percent for a car loan today.

I signed up for a time bomb—I mean, a new credit card—that charged me 23 percent interest annually. Of course, it was marketed to me as "free money," and made total sense in my head. Until I had to pay it all back.

I could have easily filed for bankruptcy, and I don't judge others who believe they must, but I knew that I had gotten myself into this mess and I needed to take responsibility and get myself out of it.

No one forced me to take on all those loans or to sign those contracts (which I did not read, even though I was encouraged to). I did that. I didn't need help screwing up my financial life. I did a brilliant job of that all by myself.

My mentor, former UN Ambassador Andrew Young, says that "men fail for three reasons: arrogance, pride, and greed."

I wasn't full of greed, but I was guilty of being full of pride. Pride kills. I needed to get over it—and get over myself.

On a related note, African Americans are the celebrated and targeted kings and queens of spending needless money, racking up more than $1 trillion in annual payouts, with almost nothing tangible to show for it.

Air Jordan tennis shoes and jeweled cell phone cases don't count. Cars don't count either—as they start depreciating the moment they drive off the lot.

In short, we don't own a THING.

It always kills me when professional athletes take out $4 million in loans to buy stuff, and then when their lives fall apart and they can't pay, now the bank is "racist" and "oppressing" them. Huh? What?

We weren't saying any of this stuff about being oppressed when we were all set to take out these ridiculous loans and credit agreements. And, no doubt, there would have been huge claims of bias and discrimination if we were denied the loans in question in the first place.

No, nine times out of ten, there is no funny business going on. We just got hoodwinked. Robbed in broad daylight. And now we're mad.

Well, while we are busy being mad and throwing up the Black Power sign or whatever, the lender just wants their money back. And unless we can prove fraud or misrepresentation, we just need to pay them. Or just say that we can't. That simple.

Losing at the roulette tables in Las Vegas does not rise to the occasion of a Dr. King writing the "Letter from a Birmingham Jail." No need to call the NAACP. They have better things to do than to waste time with someone on stupid stuff. We just need to deal with our drama. I dealt with mine.

I knew that my name was all that I had. It was my principal and primary asset. I had to protect my good name even if it hurt my pocket and my pride in the short term. I knew that my name (and my financial record) would be my signature and my calling card for the rest of my life, and I had dreams to achieve. It was time to get busy.

My credit score was once just above 500 (really bad, by the way). My credit score today is around 750. The quality of my life changed significantly when I got it above 660. Everything changed. My self-esteem, my self-confidence, and my sense of well-being, it all changed. My options expanded, and my dream making got easier.

To my personal surprise, my decision making also got *better*.

Like almost all important things in life, this was really about my own growth. This growth was simply reflected in the state of my personal credit profile and credit score. Likewise, within my own community, I believe that when our well-known reputation of our Black Consumerism is replaced by a sustained legacy of Black Wealth Accumulation—starting with raising our credit scores—we will not only see a community that has choices, a high degree of well-being, family stability, and increasing self-esteem, we will see a race that has begun to turn itself around.

Changing one's credit score isn't some game tied to "the man" trying to keep you down or "the system" oppressing you. The system didn't buy that now-broken-down television set on torn-up credit from the rent-to-own store. Knowing this is a part of getting the Memo.

Boom.

Operation HOPE Gets in the Credit-Score Game

Several years ago, Lance Triggs, one of my chief lieutenants in our silver rights movement and a dear friend who also runs a division of Operation HOPE, began experimenting with positively impacting credit scores for our adult clients. The results were stunning (to us) and liberating (to them). (Silver rights is about empowerment: How we transition beyond giving a fish and teaching how to fish to owning the boat—and the pond—itself. It is about making more money but also about making smarter financial decisions with the money we have.)

Lance and his group at Operation HOPE had consistently moved credit scores up an average of 120 points for our clients over a twenty-four-month period. The interesting thing is that in the process of raising their credit scores, they (unknowingly) accomplished so much more for the clients:

▶ Financial literacy and financial IQ improved.

▶ Confidence, personal well-being, and even self-esteem improved.

▶ Clients' options expanded and deepened, and their decision making became radically different. Even choices about who they wanted to be with as mates changed!

▶ They stopped stressing out about their lives almost overnight.

▶ They stopped reacting to whatever happened to them, and they began responding.

▶ They stopped making emotional decisions.

▸ They stopped settling and started dreaming again.

▸ They stopped being victims and began the process of taking their lives back.

In short, they began to regain control over their internal life compasses. As my friend Bill George would say, they regained their "true north." This is part and parcel of getting the Memo.

The number one cause of heart attacks, says the American Heart Association, is stress, and the number one cause of stress, ladies and gentlemen, is money. It is *all* connected. A major cause of divorce is money, too. And the number one reason why black and brown kids drop out of college is not academics, *it's money.*

Lance and our team also helped our clients build alternative credit files, often called "thick credit files," that include copies of rent statements, telephone and utility bills, insurance statements, and other legitimate forms of credit that do not show up on a traditional credit report.

When we combined our alternative credit profile work with our growing expertise to help clients lift their credit scores through traditional means, and with other powerful financial empowerment tools such as the Earned Income Tax Credit (EITC; if you make less than $50,000 a year income, you probably qualify for an EITC. Look into it!), we began to see lives change right before our eyes.

A military veteran came into one of our HOPE Inside locations in Southern California. He had been living in a homeless shelter where we were providing free financial literacy education classes. The volunteer HOPE Corps bankers whom we asked to join us for the teaching session didn't know what to expect at first. They questioned whether they were wasting their time, but my team knew it would be a customer business development opportunity for the banks—the bankers would be doing good and creating sustainable new customers at the same time!

The homeless shelter where the man temporarily lived required its clients to do three things: work, attend a financial literacy class from HOPE, and save 80 percent of their income. This gentleman was doing it all. He worked, attended classes, and he quietly saved.

A few months after our first financial literacy outing at the shelter, the same gentleman told my team he was ready to come in and open a bank account. He walked into the branch and stunned everyone when he opened a bank account valued at $50,000 cash. Boom.

Like most people, this man didn't want a hand *out*, he wanted a hand *up*. He just needed someone to believe in him. He needed someone to give him the Memo. We gave him the Memo *and* a hand up, but he surely met us more than halfway.

When you live in an economic age as we do, the issues of the day are not so much race but class. It could be argued that the important color today is not white, black, red, brown, or yellow, but green—as in the color of US currency.

In an economic world, a 700 credit score will not guarantee justice, but it can change your life. And I am not just talking about what you can buy; I'm talking about how you feel about yourself and your future. True wealth is all about how you feel about yourself.

The twenty-first-century definition of freedom is self-determination. You can change your life, starting right now. This is part of getting the Memo.

Now Buy a Home

The Memo on home ownership in America is fairly simple—
it's the tax code. The tax code in America clearly benefits the
homeowner. If you own your own home, you get mortgage
deductions that are worth their weight in gold. If you've done
your homework and built up your credit score, the US government will gladly help you pay for that house.

Mortgage tax deductions combined with regular home value
appreciation clearly establish a home purchase as your single
best hedge against poverty if you are middle class or below.

In other words, if you are a member of the Invisible Class,
becoming a homeowner is the single best way to become "seen"
in the US system of free enterprise. In one move, you become
a stakeholder, a taxpayer, an engaged citizen, and more than
likely you will now vote.

In the first years of owning your new home, almost 100
percent of your mortgage payments are tax deductible against
your income. That means that in addition to the benefit of
home ownership, you get some of your annual income back
through the mortgage deduction.

Something like 65 percent of American citizens own a
home today, but, unfortunately, many minority groups—char-
ter members of the Invisible Class—have wrongly been told
that they should not own a home. This is patently wrong. It
is really bad advice for the working poor in this country, and
possibly anywhere else.

If you want to send your kids to college, your best chance
of doing so is drawing equity from your home in twenty years
when your children are ready to go to college.

If you want to start a business or come up with down payments for your children to get on the right path by buying their own homes, then the single best chance of accomplishing this for most people is pulling accumulated equity from their homes.

Now, could this experiment of home ownership end badly? Could you end up owing more money than the home is worth? Yes, that is possible, but it is also possible that you will be dead broke in thirty years after a lifetime of work because you chose to take no risk at all. To quote Chelsea Clinton, "I would rather get caught trying to do good."

The bottom line is, if you choose to rent, you will spend X dollars per month paying off someone else's mortgage—which may be completely fine with you, by the way. Just understand what you are doing. As my friend Rod McGrew would say, "Fair exchange is no robbery."

As for me, I have no interest in freely handing over to some investor I don't know $25,000 (or an average of $2,000 in monthly rent for the typical middle-class family) or as much as $50,000 (an average annual rent in Manhattan and in other high-rent districts) of my hard-earned money so *they* can build equity in *their* real estate portfolios. For me, renting a house or apartment when I can afford to own is like opening a window and just throwing buckets of money out of it.

But it's all good if you read this and still want to rent a place to live. People like me who own single-family residential and multifamily rental real estate need for you, and a lot more like you, to keep on renting. I just want to unpack the system for you so you can decide.

In this world, you must decide whether you want to be the

one writing checks or cashing checks. An investor or a consumer. A builder or an employee. Both are good and both are necessary, but there is a mind-set difference, and it is a decision for you to make.

Homeownership works because the government made a public policy decision that it was good for America, and then folks got the Memo, so to speak. But homeownership is also as old as America itself. While mortgage interest as it relates to single family homes is relatively recent in American history, homeownership in the form of farms in the agrarian age IS America.

In fact, the ownership of private property, land, and farms is what drove these first Americans to become interested in public policy and politics. Said another way, ownership of private property was a primary reason for engagement in politics and public property.

Homeownership today is in many ways the poor person's hedge fund. Over the long arc of our history, it has been one of the best ways for the average family to both protect themselves against income erosion and to begin to build wealth.

Homeownership is part of getting the Memo.

Looking back to my years growing up in Compton, I remember one neighborhood friend and his family. My childhood friends from the Gutierrez family were lucky, as were their parents, Mr. and Mrs. Gutierrez, who immigrated from Mexico. Based on the success they witnessed growing up in Compton, my friends knew that there was a way out of the poverty we all experienced.

I remember that they owned their own home, and everyone from the family—a big family—stayed there. They worked together. They played together. They created an effective family ecosystem based on their own agreed-upon rules for aspiration and success. The rules for them were simple and straightforward: keep your nose clean; stay out of trouble; get your education; find a job (specifically, don't have a baby before you have a wife or a husband AND A JOB); save; invest; buy a home; double down on work; and, most of all, hustle.

They had their own Family Memo, and they passed it around from family member to family member until each one got it. All my friends from that family found successful paths forward, and there is no doubt in my mind that Mr. and Mrs. Gutierrez are proud of how they turned out.

But then there were other kids in the neighborhood whose families were not nearly as well put together. In fact, their families were a mess. They were renters, not owners. But, worst of all, most of the parents didn't have a Family Memo—or even realize they needed one.

Now Go Build Something

When I was coming up in Compton, California, a banker came into my classroom and taught a course in financial literacy. I remember it like it was yesterday. The entire world opened up to me when this man taught me and my classmates about what I now call the global language of money.

He wore a blue suit, a white shirt, and a red tie. I remember that it was a good suit! He happened to be Caucasian, but that didn't matter to me. He might as well have been green as far as I was concerned (as in the color of US currency).

I remember asking him, "Sir, what do you do for a living and how did you get rich—legally?" And I was dead serious.

You see, almost no one in my neighborhood wore business suits, or had a professional job with a salary for that matter. Almost everyone was an hourly wage worker. No one in my neighborhood had a business card—there were no entrepreneurs—and small business owners were in very short supply.

Anyway, the gentleman told me he was a banker and that he financed entrepreneurs. All I remember thinking was, *I don't know what an* entrepreneur *is, but I want to be one!*

I started my first business the following year at age ten, with a $40 loan, lots of love and a little encouragement from my mother, and active role modeling from my father who did in fact own a small business. Today, I am an entrepreneur and the founder of a global economic impact organization for "the least of these" called Operation HOPE, with a six-figure payroll every two weeks.

I did it playing by the rules that my mother, father, role models, society, and teachers placed in front of me, which helped in turn to create an environment where I had hope, where I could dream big dreams, and where I thrived. But for far too many in the Invisible Class—of any color and neighborhood—this story is the all-too-rare exception, not the rule. And this is the thing we must change.

Today, we need one million young people a year to decide to build something. Anything. Everything.

We need a generation of builders.

We need them to start businesses.

We need them to become entrepreneurs.

When they cannot find jobs, we need them to go create jobs for themselves.

We need one million youth a year to decide to take their lives back.

America actually needs one million small business start-ups a year to win again. We need one million start-ups a year to solve the jobs crisis in America (Gallup data). But I am not naive. I don't believe that these one million new business owners and entrepreneurs will all be successful . . . in business. Statistically, most new small business owners will fail. But so what? Success for me is about becoming resilient and building resilient people. It is about becoming positive, focused, unrelenting, and never giving up. As the saying goes, Success is going from failure to failure without loss of enthusiasm.

Success in business is not the goal. Becoming resilient is. Building leaders is. Building a Nation of Builders is.

And as we are busy doing this—nurturing a new generation of positive, confident, affirming leaders and builders—we are bound to find one (or more) new Steve Jobs or Reginald Lewis (look him up) in our urban and rural communities. And THIS is our magic sauce.

The reality is that every big business was once a small one.

All of us with manicured nails had generations before us, foremothers and forefathers, with dirt underneath their nails. They were not "proper" people at the dining room table, but they may have made the dining room table! They certainly made it possible for all of us today to sit at the dining room table. But we forget about all of that.

We assume that rich people have always been rich. Not true.

Or that poor people are destined to always be poor. This does not have to be true.

The fact is that America and most of the free world were built by entrepreneurs and dreamers, most of whom started out poor and unsophisticated.

What was Walmart if not a man named Sam Walton with a high school education, a storefront, and a pickup truck? From that humble beginning, he built the largest retailer in the world that is today the largest employer of African Americans, seniors, and women in the world.

What was UPS (United Parcel Service) if not the vision of one man named Jim Casey with $100 and a bicycle? UPS is today not only a global logistics company with 400,000 employees, it is also one of the world's ten largest airlines.

What were *Ebony* and *Jet* magazines if not a bet made by a young John H. Johnson, who borrowed $500 from his mother to start what is now one of the largest publishing empires serving Black America? The same can be said for Earl Graves, another black man with a dream, who started *Black Enterprise* magazine, or as I call it, the black *Wall Street Journal*. And for Edward Lewis, his partners, and my friend Susan Taylor, who together built *Essence* magazine from a dream into a brand so important and valuable that Time Warner paid many millions to buy it.

But we have lost these storylines in our lives. We think that all big companies have always been big, and we simply want to work there.

A recent *USA Today* poll found that the majority of youth want to graduate from college and go work for a small handful of big, well-known companies, companies that for the most part are *not hiring*. Not because they have something against you, but simply because big companies are not—as relates to their growth—in the people-hiring business. They are in the efficiency business. And efficiency at that size and scale comes much more from technology than it comes from people.

But who does love people enough to hire them? Small businesses and entrepreneurs do, that's who.

Most of the new job growth in America and the world over comes from entrepreneurs, small businesses, start-ups and shoot-ups, in years three to seven.

Half of all companies in America have 100 employees or less, according to Gallup. About 70 percent of all companies in America are 500 employees or less.

And fewer than 1,000 businesses in America employ more than 10,000 people—so few you can name them.

If you're ready to build something of your own, Operation HOPE is here to help you get there, and plenty of others are, too. If you feel like you are already an entrepreneur, feel free to skip to Rule 4 and learn how to create your own economy that works for you.

Why Your Free Enterprise Isn't Just Your Concern

I hope I've planted a seed that helps you see the power of simple financial goals like improving your credit score, buying a house, and starting a business. More than anything, I want you to succeed, but I'd be wrong if I stopped there. This book isn't about just you escaping the Invisible Class, but about all of us—our neighbors, our communities, and our churches—doing that.

Your financial health is directly related to your power, safety, and future, but also to the power, safety, and future of your community. If you don't believe me, travel with me to Ferguson, Missouri.

Ferguson was dying in 2014 after the death of Michael Brown, but quite possibly not just for the reasons you might believe.

First, please don't take anything I say below about Ferguson's economy and businesses as minimizing Michael Brown's tragic death and his family's loss or the town's failures to dispense justice and opportunity equally to all. That's plenty of work for another book. Ferguson needs equal justice and equal rights, but I think it's also high time we addressed the things that are dying in Ferguson that do not appear in the evening news or protest signs.

I am talking about the death of small business and jobs and, with it, the resiliency of both a people and a community in a once-vibrant American city.

I'm not talking here about big government jobs or even big business jobs or even big business for that matter. I'm not talking about the so-called evil capitalists who control billions and order our lives from afar. I'm not even talking about the businesses that played a negative role in creating an environment of crisis, such as was the case during the Rodney King riots of 1992.

I'm talking about mom-and-pop small business owners—including gas stations, convenience stores, and hair salons—four million of the six million businesses in America that employ one person or more across the nation.

I'm talking about small businesses that take in $100,000 annually on average, maybe $250,000 in a very good year, and as a result of this, enable the owners to put roofs over their children's heads and food on the table, send their kids to college, pay their taxes, and go on vacation once a year. These are the capitalists responsible for more than 70 percent of all businesses in America and the vast majority around the world. They look like you and me, and destroying them destroys us too.

Some examples of these small businesses in Ferguson were:

The Quick Trip: burned down during the first Michael Brown demonstration.

The Ferguson Market: looted the next night.

The beloved Red's BBQ, a recognized and well-respected community institution: looted and shut down.

None of these and the many other small businesses affected by the demonstrations had anything to do with the injustices taking place in Ferguson, but several would never open again. Some didn't even have a desire to come back. This community, which had few jobs to speak of before the Michael Brown crisis, had significantly fewer after everything went down.

And what Ferguson, especially the youth of Ferguson, needs almost as much as they feel the need for social and criminal justice, are JOBS. Just listen to what eleven-year-old Marquis Govan told the St. Louis Commission, which was looking into this crisis: "We don't need more tear gas, we need jobs" ("Meet an 11-Year-Old Voice of Reason," CBS News, September 21, 2014, http://www.cbsnews.com/news/meet-an-11-year-old-voice-of-reason/). Brilliance and solutions, from one of Ferguson's future leaders.

But how is anyone supposed to know what they really need (jobs) and how to get them in a place like Ferguson? The fact is, these most recent and well-meaning residents of Ferguson, Missouri, never got the Memo. Nearly one in four people living there are below the poverty line, and the rate of home owner-ship is the lowest in the state.

This lack of understanding of America's free-enterprise system and of how to create a sustainable life for oneself is not only driving unemployment (and crime along with it) in places like Ferguson, it also explains why a young man with an otherwise bright future, like Michael Brown, took a few cigars from a store instead of finding a way to pay for them.

The people who called Ferguson home for the past hundred years, up until about 2000, actually had the Memo. They got it from their mothers and fathers, their mentors, and their friends who were homeowners and business owners. And, unfortunately, most of these longtime residents also control the seats of power in Ferguson's government and criminal jus-tice system, too—we now know that a police department that doesn't reflect the cultural or racial makeup of the neighbor-hoods they protect can lead to big problems.

When you better understand the plight of those who never got the Memo, it is easier to see how it leads to low employ-ment, low quality of life, communities in need of resources, and consequently crime and looting. The facts and statistics behind the real Ferguson are nothing less than stunning. Here is just one—Ferguson, Missouri, represents the widest racial gap of the unbanked in the entire nation, according to the Federal Deposit Insurance Corporation.

And so, yes, we must pursue our social justice agenda in Ferguson, but we must also stop killing the geese that lay all the golden eggs: small businesses and the entrepreneurial spirit. And not only in Ferguson, but in each and every stabilized community here and around the world.

Remember, a broke person cannot help the poor of Ferguson escape their own poverty. Or, to quote the late Shimon Peres (former Israeli prime minister and president), when I last saw him in Jordan: "Even if you want to distribute money like a socialist, you have to first start collecting money like a capitalist."

We live in a free-enterprise capitalist system. It's time to embrace it.

Your Mind-Set Makes or Loses Money and Wealth—You Choose

Before you can be the CEO of anybody else, you must be the best CEO of YOU.

The reality is that YOU are capital. All wealth—and all poverty—begins with you. In fact, it begins *within* you, with the knowledge in your head and your heart and your soul. With your mind-set.

I believe that fully half of modern poverty—beyond basic issues of sustenance of course—is tied to a poor mind-set, to low self-esteem and a lack of confidence. Because if you don't feel good about yourself, no one else will. Because if you don't know who you are at 9 a.m., by dinnertime someone is going to tell you who you are. And bad things will come after that.

Here are some universal truths:

If I don't like me, I am not going to like you.

If I don't respect me, I don't have a clue how to respect you.

If I don't love me, I don't know how to love you.

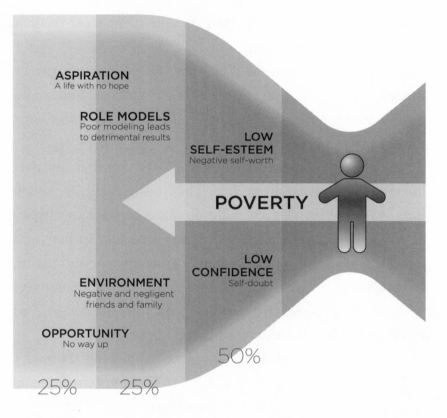

And it naturally follows, if I don't have a purpose in my life, I am going to turn your life into a living hell.

Whatever goes around, comes around. We reap what we sow.

This is why I hammer so hard on the issue of self-esteem and confidence. Because it is the beginning of everything.

According to my HOPE Doctrine on Poverty, the second part of poverty is crappy role models and a crappy environment. The causes of poverty are illustrated in the figure.

Why do so many urban kids think that the highest possible aspiration they should have in life is to become a drug dealer, a rap star, or an athlete? It is because those are the aspirational images of success (crappy role models) that exist in the neighborhoods where they grew up and spent most of their time (crappy environment).

Everyone is aspirational. Everyone. These kids are simply modeling themselves on what they see as success. And so, we need to give them something better to see so they know what they can truly be.

No one wakes in the morning and says that their greatest life ambition is to be on welfare. That young family is modeling themselves on a legacy of family elders on welfare, a legacy of not getting the Memo. There is not a mother in her right mind who does not want her child to grow up to be successful, hardworking, and taxpaying, if for no other reason than to feel pride. But you cannot give your kids what you do not have. And if you don't know better, you cannot do better.

In the absence of wisdom, ignorance happily fills the void.

Out of love, we pass down bad habits from generation to generation. I repeat: we do this out of love . . .

No woman wakes up in the morning and says that her greatest ambition in life is to be a prostitute. She is modeling what she sees as the symbols of aspiration in her neighborhood. She is also doing it for money. There is no other legitimate, continuing motivation to do it. Remove the financial aspect, and the entire global prostitution industry dies within a month.

It is what we don't know that we don't know—but we *think* we know—that is killing us.

And then you have the issue of environment. The best way to summarize this problem is: If you hang around nine broke people, you will be the tenth. But if you grow up with nine nuclear scientists, you will also likely be the tenth.

When you are poor and struggling—and everyone around

you is poor and struggling—and when you don't feel good about yourself, and your hope dies, you are not just skeptical, you are cynical. And once you become cynical, you are done. It is only a matter of time before you fail. You've already given up on yourself, so you can't see the opportunities. Your worldview is through a negative lens, and your glass of life is half empty.

"Whether you think you can or think you can't, you're right."
—HENRY FORD

Mind-set matters.

The HOPE Doctrine on Wealth

Growing up in Compton and South Central Los Angeles, I hung around with people who were doers and owners, positive folks who told me they loved me on a regular basis. As a result, today I consider myself a doer. I am an owner, I am positive, and I love myself. I am not a rocket scientist; I benefited from the assets of my environment, and I have been role modeling myself.

Truth be told, the greatest asset of my life was learning to love myself, whole and complete. My most important accomplishment was reaching a point where I became "reasonably comfortable" in my own skin. I believe this should be everyone's goal.

Mind-set matters. A positive mind-set naturally leads to having aspirations for our lives. *Aspiration* is a code word for hope, and hope leads to a sense of opportunity, a view of the world through the lens of possibilities, where the glass is always half full. Hope is the beginning of true wealth, which I dig into even deeper in Rule 5.

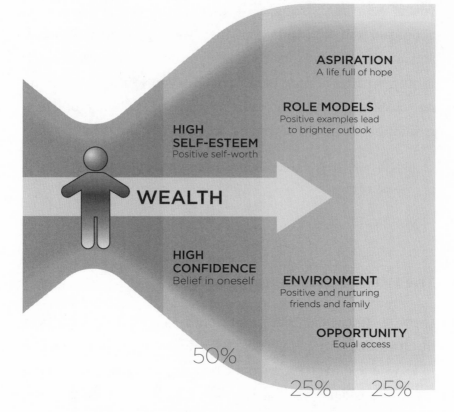

True wealth, like true poverty, has nothing to do with money. True wealth is illustrated in the figure.

In short, here is what the wealthy have:

▶ They have high self-esteem and a high level of self-confidence.

▶ They wake up in the morning believing that they can.

▶ They have positive role models and are raised in an empowering environment.

▶ They have hope and are optimistic about life.

▶ They see opportunity everywhere.

How We Choose to Be Wealthy (or Not)

The ability to see opportunity everywhere is a key factor separating those in the Invisible Class who can build financial success and economic wealth from those who end up truly poor in aspiration. Let me explain.

I started the book talking about a video I recorded titled "Modern Slavery." In the video, I paint a picture of a modern poor community, one where you see a check casher, next to a payday loan lender, next to rent-to-own store, next to a liquor store, etcetera.

I explain how people in the Invisible Class are being robbed in broad daylight, but almost no one does anything about it. They see these things as normal and do nothing to expel these businesses from their communities, while railing against other forms of perceived oppression such as police brutality and the loss of blue-collar jobs.

Meanwhile, those who are "wealthy" in their thinking drive through those communities, and they see in run-down homes an opportunity to buy, rehabilitate, upgrade, and rent them to working residents.

Think about the Korean family who has established a hair care store selling hair weaves exclusively to African American women (this example is particularly jaw-dropping to me) in a majority black neighborhood. There is absolutely nothing wrong with the Korean family doing this—except that black residents of the same community should have done it first. Simply put, black folks should have seen the opportunity to create a successful business that serves their community first.

Instead, because of their poverty mind-set, they have been locked out of their own market.

When you have a "poor" outlook on life, you miss seeing the opportunities in front of you. You miss getting the Memo.

Take any number of business establishments that set up shop in poor and underserved communities. They are not sneaking into these communities in the dead of night. They are not stealing from someone and setting up illegal enterprises. They are not hoodwinking anyone. They simply got the Memo: They saw the opportunity, they believed in themselves and in their entrepreneurial abilities, and they took action. They invested time, energy, and resources believing they would get a return on investment.

Take those who walk right into your neighborhood and buy centrally located real estate for pennies on the dollar, transforming the neighborhood in time from a poor community to a gentrified, upwardly mobile, economically vibrant, new-age middle-class enclave. These are people who got the Memo.

Don't hate. Those who do this are worthy of commendation. Remember, the best revenge is living well.

Look at what's happening in Detroit and in Harlem.

Detroit is coming back. It's a fact. The question is not whether Detroit is coming back but rather who is Detroit coming back for and when?

Downtown Detroit has already been claimed by a generation of upwardly mobile, college-educated young people who think that living in downtown lofts and starting small shops and owning restaurants there is a cool thing to do.

When you walk into a clothing shop in downtown Detroit and you see someone selling $300 T-shirts in 2016, then you know two things to be true: (1) Something is happening in Detroit. (2) Someone else has gotten the Memo.

And for years officials would have given you property in Harlem for next to nothing. But today a teardown in Harlem is $750,000—when you can find one. Brownstones sell for $1 million and more today. The black community responds by asking, "What happened to our black community?"

Those who got the Memo didn't see a black community in Harlem. They saw Manhattan as what it is: an island, complete with the Upper East Side, the Upper West Side, Lower Manhattan, and what we call Harlem, with Central Park in the center of it all.

They saw white people (on the Upper East Side of Manhattan), white people (on the Upper West Side of Manhattan), white people (in Lower Manhattan)—and black people in Harlem.

After a while, with increasing wealth, a growing population, and limited land, white folks began to say, "Black folks aren't so bad." And then, smartly, they began moving into Harlem. They brought with them their businesses and their lifestyles, and they made it cool for their friends to do the same. And now Harlem is nothing more than upper Manhattan. Once again.

Hear this: Those who got the Memo didn't see a black community; they saw centrally located real estate. And by the time the black community figured out what was going on, it was way too late.

The deals are gone. Property values are through the roof, and we find ourselves priced out of yet another market. In our own neighborhood. A place that had been our neighborhood for over a hundred years. And not knowing anything different, we see this as yet another example of inequality, injustice, gentrification, possibly even racism and discrimination. In reality, we simply never got the Memo.

And there you have it.

Do you know how the Bible describes poverty? In Proverbs 10:4, the Bible says, "Lazy hands make a man poor, but diligent hands bring wealth." Maybe your pastor forgot to tell you about that verse.

Yes, the members of the Invisible Class are sent into the modern economic marketplace with systemic handicaps: crappy self-esteem, crappy role models, no knowledge of economics or how money works, and no hope, as a bonus.

But in order to move forward, we must take ownership of ourselves. We must find a way to heal, to learn to love ourselves, and thereafter to love each other, to get ourselves out of this mess. Otherwise, we can never truly be free.

The new slavery is not shackles or police handcuffs on our arms and legs. These are shackles and handcuffs on our hearts, our minds, and our souls.

The new wealth is about healing and believing. It is about a mind-set that sees opportunity—and that gets the Memo.

Okay, CEO of YOU: Step Up

Increasingly you are on your own.

Employment is no longer a thirty-year, single-employer career promise as maybe your mother or father or grandmother or uncle enjoyed. Most employees today will work as many as a half-dozen different jobs in the course of their working lives—sometimes a combination of two or more jobs at the same time.

You are on your own.

With major companies merging, one person rather than two may be needed for the same position, so fewer people will work for big companies over time.

You are on your own.

Small businesses and entrepreneurs overwhelmingly employ the most people in the United States and the world over, but (at least here in the United States) we now have for the first time more small business deaths than small business births. What we need is a small business revolution, and what we have are small businesses in active retreat.

You are on your own.

You can scream, holler, wish, hope, or pray if you like (well, we should *all* pray). You can cry victim—you can even file a formal grievance somewhere. But no one is coming to save you.

Everyone today has problems, and increasingly no one cares. Am I trying to depress you? No, I am trying to wake you up. You see, no one is coming to save you. You are going to have to do that for yourself.

God may love you in heaven, but here on earth you must save yourself.

The fact is, most of us have the same problem. Large sections of the working class and middle class the world over are entering the Invisible Class. These people are seeing their comfortable standard of living and, even worse in their eyes, their very way of life slowly deteriorating and slipping away. They are increasingly resentful about the state of the world and, as a result, are markedly less compassionate than, say, their parents and grandparents before them. These are not bad people. They are almost all very good people. But they are stressed out and worried, which makes people narrowly focused and (understandably) more self-absorbed. This speaks to the recent election results.

If I were white and high school educated, seeing my once-stable blue-collar economy of fifty-plus years falling away, I would feel invisible and frustrated, too. But—just like with our depressed urban areas—instead of going in and helping these small-town communities to reimagine and reset their local economies, we let them drift into sadness and obsolescence.

When we should have helped to revitalize the economies of these beautiful small towns, we ignored them. We hoped that their problems would solve themselves, but of course they actually got worse—so bad that like the upset urban poor and people of color in America, poor whites wanted a spokes-man too. Enter a man as a presidential candidate, viewed by a majority of this disenfranchised group as a man in charge of the "Anger Party" and a vessel of articulated frustration for poor white male pain in America.

All of this and more underlines the truth that you are increasingly on your own in this world.

Governments are broke.

Resources are increasingly limited.

Quality education is increasingly expensive and increasingly favors the well connected. It could even be argued that public education is increasingly becoming a private amenity.

The middle class is financially strapped, and the working class is beginning to feel poor.

In this developing environment, being a victim—legitimate or not—will not save you. You must now save yourself.

This is the era in which people must learn to not only do

for themselves but to truly empower themselves, to chart the economic course for their own lives.

This is the beginning of the empowerment age.

What About Public Assistance?

Sympathy: the feeling that you care about and are sorry about someone else's trouble, grief, misfortune, etcetera.

Empathy: the feeling that you understand and share another person's experiences and emotions; the ability to share someone else's feelings.

People in the Invisible Class—the poor, the struggling, the underserved, the left behind, and the pushed aside—need less sympathy in the twenty-first century and much more of what I call "modern empathy." Let me explain.

Remember when I said that if I gave a homeless man $1 million, he would be broke within six months? It's not a moral issue, and it has nothing to do with whether I like the homeless man or not. It does not have anything to do with a bias toward the homeless or a bias against giving out pure charity (I am a fan of pure charity, for the record).

It's not about race or racism (note that I have not even mentioned a race for the homeless man in this example). It is not about my good intentions, or yours. In fact, it is important to remove any sense of guilt out of this hypothetical example and the decisions associated with it. Any decision you make emotionally, I guarantee you, will be a bad one.

The simple fact is that the homeless man was homeless for a reason, be it for mental, physical, emotional, financial, or other problems. We need to empathize with the man and his plight in order to be in a position to assist him on the road to economic liberation.

But that is not what happened here. In this hypothetical example, I felt sorry for the man, and so—maybe even to feel better about myself and my own shortcomings—I gave the man $1 million and wished him well.

In this example, there was almost no way for the man to be successful. He would have been broke within six months because nothing changed in his head, where most poverty actually begins. Without financial literacy, one finds out very quickly that an uninformed rich person and their wallet are soon separated.

And no different than the person who won the lottery and ended up broke or the professional athlete with a $100 million contract who ended up broke, this man would soon have found a large and growing group of "family and friends" to help him spend his newly gotten gains on things that did not add to his future wealth and well-being.

What the world needs now is less sympathy and more empathy. Public assistance is keeping many of us alive out of sympathy, but it is not giving any of us the power to be free and independent. And we all know it can be taken away in an instant depending on political fortunes or chance.

What the world needs now is less of a hand *out* and more of a hand *up*.

Beyond giving the men and women of the Invisible Class fish—or even teaching them how to fish—there needs to be a new national focus on showing them how to own the bait and boat, and thereafter how to own the lake, too.

We need to make sure we are applying care on the level of human dignity, the version of welfare that dates back to the Roman Empire, and thereafter adopted by the early Chinese, European, and other world leaders. I'm talking about taking care of our elderly, taking care of our children, and taking care of our disabled and others who cannot take care of themselves.

To this day, African Americans as a percentage of their population utilize public assistance to a much greater degree than whites and at a slightly higher rate than our Latino brothers and sisters. Asians, interestingly enough, use very little formal public assistance. This probably has more to do with a culture of deep support within the extended family among various Asian race groups.

It is for this reason that I believe that my community in particular simply did not get the Memo. We are not creating sustainable wealth, our own jobs, and our own economic base, and that is not because of a lack of talent. Everywhere that African Americans focus their talent and energy, they succeed (for example, in music, entertainment, professional sports, and the arts).

We are not dumb and we are not stupid. It is what we don't know that we don't know—but that we think we know—that is killing us.

A Fish Story

Someone once told me this story.

> A man is sitting on the porch of his ramshackle home, facing a lake.
>
> A community developer visiting the community said to

the man, "You seem very able. Have you ever thought about getting a boat and fishing in that lake?" The man responded, "Well, why do that?"

The community developer then said, "Because if you fished and did well, you could sell your caught fish to the local markets, and then buy a larger boat." The man responded, "Well, why do that?"

The community developer then said, "Because if you did that you could hire some of your friends, creating jobs, and maybe someday buy a fleet of boats." The man responded, "Well, why do that?"

The community developer, growing frustrated, then said, "Because if you did that you could become a community hero and a major employer in your own community." The man responded, "Well, why do that?"

The community developer, now totally flustered and out of options, said, "Because if you built wealth and did all this, you could then relax and retire yourself for the rest of your days, doing what you love, sitting on your porch." The man then responded, "Well, I am already doing that!"

Sad, but funny.

How you choose to live your life is a choice. Improve your odds and choose the mind-set of wealth.

Your Relationships Are Investments— Build Relationship Capital with Yourself First

I have spent a good portion of this book focused on helping you to get pointed in the right direction and to be well positioned for your own success. Why? Because there is no more important relationship than the one you have with yourself. Everything else in your life pivots off that relationship.

The relationship between you and yourself will be the first in the hopefully long and growing line of relationship capital in your life. This is why the most important commitment I made early on in my career was to become "reasonably comfortable" in my own skin.

The reality is that no one is totally comfortable in their own skin. That is perfection, and perfection simply does not exist. Perfection is an illusion, and we all just need to get over that and move on, living the best and most authentic lives we can.

We all know people who go through the vast majority of their lives striving to project an image of perfection. Not only is this "pretending to be perfect" thing not in any way convincing, it actually stresses the person in question out. They get stressed, and if it continues, they will get older and less healthy quicker. Why? Because your body is made of 70 percent water, and when you get hot and bothered all the time—stressed, upset, angry, highly negative, and negatively charged—you are theoretically "cooking" your organs. Done repeatedly, over time, it simply isn't healthy.

That means that authenticity matters.

Sincerity and character matter.

Integrity matters.

Most of all, it means that genuine care matters. People can pick up on inauthentic energy in a split second, and when that happens, you can forget about doing business with them. They get that nagging sense that they are simply being used, and no one wants to feel used.

But you don't have to worry about inauthentic energy when you develop an open and honest first relationship with yourself. Consider the wisdom embedded in the South African word *ubuntu*. "I am me because you are you." Or as they say in Rwandan, *agaciro*, which means "dignity." The more you know about yourself, the more you have to offer someone else.

Relationship Capital Made Simple

All wealth—financial and otherwise—is built upon relationships. Think about it. If I gave you $1 billion and put you on a desert island, that money would be worthless. Your mental, spiritual, and financial capital is valuable only to the extent that you can share it and spend it with others. The more people with whom you can share and build capital, the more you have what I call "relationship capital."

Your level of legitimate trust in any real relationship determines the amount of capital you have. If you are a criminal brute forcing people to do what you want out of fear and intimidation, then that is not what I am talking about (nor is it sustainable).

If you have a friend who "borrows" $20 every week but never returns it, you will eventually distrust him, and you will not continue to "lend" him money. His relationship capital will be zero. Financial experts give businesses fancy investment ratings—basically credit scores—but this is exactly the same thing as grading your ability to trust your friend to repay you. A credit score is just a mathematical way of determining how much relationship capital you would have if you asked a banker to lend you some of his money.

Think about your current relationship capital with yourself. Do you keep your promises? Do you step up for what matters to you? Do you trust yourself to do the right thing when the time comes? Are you honest and trustworthy even when nobody is looking? Believing in yourself is the first step toward building relationship capital with others.

Who Is in Your Circle of Influence?

This is a BIG and important question.

► Whom do you hang around with?
► Whom do you choose to spend quality time with?
► Where do you invest time and energy?

▶ Whom do you associate with at work and play?

▶ Which family members are you attracted to and use as role models?

▶ Are you curating your life or just reacting through it?

▶ Why does any of this matter?

Because, like I've said before, if you hang around nine broke people, you will be the tenth. You are—or will become—the person you hang around with.

The world works in a series of concentric circles. Circles of wealth, power, education, access, and opportunity not only swirl within the same concentric circle rings, or sets of related and connected rings, they also build on themselves. They feed on each other.

On a recent business day in Atlanta, I met with the CEO of the Metro Atlanta Chamber of Commerce, Hala Moddelmog, and her team in their office. Both of our offices are now located within the same building in Atlanta. I later found out that other people in my office had separately visited with other leaders in her office earlier that same day, having nothing to do with either her or me.

Later that same day I met with the chairman and CEO of SunTrust Banks Atlanta, Allison Dukes, whom I discovered was also meeting with Hala later that same day, along with the head of a major area foundation with offices in the same building as Operation HOPE.

And how did I meet Allison Dukes? At a dinner with one of my friends and business heroes, Bill Rogers, chairman and CEO of all of SunTrust Banks, and someone who has become a linchpin in the acceptance and explosive growth of the HOPE

Inside franchise nationwide. Because he is a big-time, top-10 bank CEO, other top-100 CEOs accept me on his unspoken word. It is the way these concentric circles work.

And how did I meet Bill? Well, it was through another one of my heroes and friends, Jim Wells, the former chairman and CEO of SunTrust Banks. Jim Wells made the first big SunTrust bet on my dreams.

And how did I meet Jim Wells? Through Scott Wilfong of SunTrust Banks and Steve Bartlett, the former Dallas mayor and former congressman who was, at the time of the introduction, CEO of the Financial Services Roundtable (FSR). And I originally met Steve and the FSR family through Don McGrath, the then CEO of Bank of the West. Bill Rogers and Jim Wells both serve on our HOPE executive board today. Are you getting the Memo?

Success in life is not just about how smart you are, or whether there is a need, or whether you are deserving. The world operates in a flow, and you must get yourself into the right FLOW. You do that by building relationship capital.

Essentially, the Memo says: Get out of your comfort zone and form relationships in the places where you want to be. The more you connect with higher-capital people, the higher you raise your own capital worth.

If you grew up around wealthy people—went to school with children of influence, went to camp with these same kids, and grew up with them and grew up going to club events and traveling in the "upper cabin" of the airplane (business or first class)—then you sort of naturally cultivate those kinds of relationships as well as the culture of those spaces, people, and places.

If you grew up around smart kids, liked after-school projects, were drawn to research, loved your homework, joined nerdy clubs, hung out in STEM (science, technology, engineering, and math) environments, and cultivated mentors who looked like what you wanted to become, well, then you end up cultivating those sorts of relationships and adopting the culture and norms of those spaces, people, and places.

But if you grew up around thugs, crooks, drug dealers, and drug addicts, wannabe gangbangers, regulars at strip clubs, kids who thought it was cool to drop out of school in tenth grade, and you are surrounded by a whole series of predatory businesses—check cashers, payday lenders, title lenders, and liquor stores—then you naturally end up cultivating those relationships and adopting the culture and norms of those spaces, people, and places.

Just like wealth circles tie into wealth circles, so can poverty circles tie directly into other poverty circles, creating endless concentric circles of poverty and despair and depressed relationships that are hard to escape. They become all that you see, quite literally.

I did not grow up around privilege, opportunity, and power. I grew up in the hood. My mother worked a union job for McDonnell Douglas as a fabricator, and my dad ran his own small business doing cement contracting. I was not part of any elite access club. In fact, I was homeless for six months when I was eighteen years old and was forced to basically start over from nothing. But I knew I had talents and gifts. I just needed to cultivate them in the right way and in the right environment. So, I decided to create my own environment. I decided to create my own culture.

If no one would mentor me, I would track down and recruit my own mentors, and ask them to invest fifteen minutes with me every few weeks. Now who would turn down a fifteen-minute request of their time once a month?

How I Chased Down Ambassador Young

People hear me talk all the time about civil rights icon Ambassador Andrew Young as my mentor, personal hero, and friend. He is all of that, and close to a father figure in my life at this point as well, but there was a time when he had not a clue who I was and was not all that interested in learning more. To state it kindly, I was a pest of the highest order. I would just never give up.

I would find out where Andrew Young was speaking, and I would drive or fly there, depending on the distance. Yes, I said fly there. At my own expense. I would hustle the money up, and I would purchase a plane ticket—with no advance appointment or guarantee to meet him.

I did this in countless cities for over a decade. Wherever he was, that is where I wanted to be. Why? Because he and Quincy Jones were the only two black men I knew of in the whole, entire world who were "international."

These two men were not black leaders who traveled places. They were internationally respected global leaders. Absolute best in class in their fields. Who also happened to be black. They were not "black for a living," but they were very proud to be black. This, I decided, was my model.

And so, I did tons of research on Young, showed genuine and authentic interest, and then I made an investment in the relationship. I would show up wherever he happened to be. But I was not stalking the man. If he could not meet with me, or if he didn't even have time to speak with me, that was okay. He owed me nothing. This was a risk that I was willing to take—for me and my future. One day I got lucky.

I heard that Ambassador Andrew Young was keynoting at a Corporate Council on Africa meeting in Dallas, Texas, so I purchased a plane ticket, registered for the conference, and flew there. Believe me, every purchase back then was a struggle. I decided to purchase a plane ticket instead of wasting money on a weekend of partying in the Los Angeles club scene. I decided to purchase a ticket instead of a stereo or cool rims for my car, which is where most of my friends my age were pouring their cash.

When I showed up in Dallas, Andrew Young had come down with a bug. He had to speak soon, but he was not feeling well. I decided that this was my chance. I offered to put him in my car and drive him to the pharmacy to get him whatever he needed. It worked, and for forty-five minutes, on the way to and on the way back from the pharmacy, I had this man's undivided attention. I had borrowed my friend Effie Booker's Mercedes Benz automobile to drive Young around. It worked like a charm except for one thing—he didn't remember anything I said to him. His mind was somewhere else.

I had all but given up when I decided to try one more time. I flew in to the annual dinner for the Joint Center for Political and Economic Studies in Washington, DC, where once again Young was the speaker. I thought he might still have no clue who I was, and I was okay with that. I had tried. But a friend of mine, Robert McNeely of Union Bank of California, wanted to meet Young. I could at least try to make an introduction. And so, after the dinner I took Robert over to meet Young. To my surprise, Young then introduced me to his son, Andrew "Bo" Young III. Today, Bo Young and I are the best of friends. Very much like brothers.

Truth be told, if not for Bo Young needling me, I would not have the relationship that I have with his father today. The funniest call I can remember receiving was Bo calling me in California one day and asking, "Hey man, why don't you like my daddy? Why haven't you ever asked me to introduce you to him so you two could have a real conversation about community change?"

I was dumbfounded. If he only knew what I had gone through all those years. But I sucked it up and just said, "You're right. I would love to meet your father." Within a few days, I was again on a plane, this time to Atlanta. The agenda was lunch with Bo and Andrew Young.

Now, I would love to say here that we had lunch and everything clicked, but such is the furthest thing from the truth. We had our lunch, and once again, I outlined my vision for Operation HOPE, my proposed silver rights movement, and community change. It felt like I had been talking into a wind tunnel. Lunch was over, and Young had to run back to his office for a media interview. But then, at the last moment, he turned to me and asked, "What are you plans after lunch?"

I said, "Nothing," even though I had a packed schedule. He invited me to come over to his office to continue our conversation, and so I cancelled everything else I had scheduled that day.

I went to Andrew Young's office after lunch, and we had a

five-hour conversation. On my way out of his office, he stopped and showed me a one-of-a-kind painting from a Nigerian prince. He asked me if I liked it, and then he pulled it off the wall and gave it to me. That was it. I fell in love with the man that day, and he went on to become our global spokesman for Operation HOPE.

Young was not in my circle. I curated an environment in which Young's circle could cross mine, and because of that my circle has significantly expanded.

As I said before, the Memo says: Get out of your comfort zone and form relationships in the places where you want to be. The more you connect with higher-capital people, the higher you raise your own capital worth.

I have basically been doing this my entire life, building relationship capital. It is part of what makes me, me. It is part of the magic sauce. It is part of getting the Memo.

The way I met Quincy Jones was equally bizarre. I decided that I wanted to have a relationship with Q, to be mentored by him, to model myself on his life. But I did not know him. He was a legend surrounded by a dozen handlers, and I was this young kid from the hood (albeit assertive), who like millions of other kids wanted to know the man who made Michael Jackson what he ultimately became. This is where that quote from my late mentor and friend Dr. Dorothy I. Height comes in. She told me one day, "John, I like you because you are a dreamer with a shovel in your hands."

One day an invite came across my desk for a fund-raiser for a congresswoman from California. I couldn't care less about the fund-raiser, but it was being held at the home of none other than one Quincy Delight Jones!

This congresswoman was a nice enough person, but I did not really know her. And, truth be told, the entire Congressional Black Caucus group (CBC) from California was kind of indifferent toward me back then. I received $1 million in federal appropriations from a member of the Hispanic Caucus (led by Congresswoman Lucille Roybal-Allard), but the CBC was not really interested in me, for whatever strange reason. One member was actually openly hostile toward me. And so, I knew they would lift not one finger to help me meet Q. But with $1,000 in my hands, I could meet him myself. I just had to show up to the fund-raiser.

I made it my business to land a new consulting client over those next couple of weeks with the sole aim of securing an advance retainer of $1,000—the same $1,000 I would use to get access to Q's home. The problem for me back then, however, was that I was a social misfit. I was keen in business, but I had few social skills in large groups. I was a social introvert—unless you were talking about business or life missions. And so, I went to the fund-raiser at Q's home and proceeded to hold up a wall, nursing a glass of Coca-Cola with melting ice.

About the time I was getting ready to leave, the oddest thing happened: I heard someone calling my name. It wasn't just any old someone calling my name, it was Quincy Jones himself! He was in the next room, and I heard him asking the congresswoman, since deceased (God rest her soul), whether she knew me. He had heard about my work with HOPE after the riots, and he wanted to meet me. Get that: Q wanted to meet ME! I had to keep myself from laughing out loud when I heard the congresswoman bragging to Q about "what a wonderful young man I was," like we were buddies. But that's Hollywood for you, so I just smiled and played along. I was focused on only one thing: meeting Q.

I was ushered over, and Q put his arm around my shoulder—and for everyone in that room I was a made man for the rest of the evening. But I don't remember much about anyone else that night because Q pulled me over into a corner of his home, and we spoke nonstop for the next seven hours. When I looked up, all the guests had departed. It was just Q and me. And as I was leaving, he gave me all his private contact details. We have been connected at the spiritual hip ever since.

I have now joined Q all over the world, from Montreux, Switzerland, to Manhattan, New York City, and back. But, hands down, our best and richest times have been just sharing stories about the world and laughter about ourselves right in his inspiring Bel Air living room. What a man he is. And I am honored to call him a mentor and a friend.

But what if I hadn't taken the initiative? What if I hadn't made the investment of time, energy, and resources? What if I didn't have the right spirit, if I had chosen to not tolerate the people standing between me and him and who meant me no good? Everything would be different. But now Q and I are connected, and through him my circles of influence have expanded tenfold, just as they did when I connected with Andrew Young.

Who are you hanging around?

Who are your family members hanging around?

Do you want to be like the people in this group?

If not, then you must change what you and they see. Starting today.

This is part of getting the Memo.

Networking Is Not Relationship Building

So maybe you think my chasing people like Andrew Young, Quincy Jones, and Jack Kemp (I left that story out . . .) around the country is a form of networking. Let me explain why I don't think so.

There is a big difference between networking and relationship building. In fact, networking does not generate relationship capital at all. For anything other than the barter, trade, and transactions of the most basic needs, most traditional networking is not even very helpful.

Networking is about "What do I get?" Relationship building is about "What do I have to give?"

Networking is a *taking* not a *giving* business. When someone is handing you their business card at a networking event, they are busy asking themselves, "So what can I get from this guy or woman?" And then what do we do with all the business cards that we receive at networking events? Shove them all in a drawer never to be looked at again.

Let me tell you something that few others will. No one who can really help you advance your station in life—or, more bluntly, no one of substance—goes to networking receptions. Now, am I saying that all networking events are useless? Absolutely not. My friend George Fraser of FraserNet is a good example of the exception to the rule.

George does not throw networking events; he uses networked opportunities to "educate-up" and to empower those that make the investment and choose to show up. More so, George is an ongoing resource to everyone who connects with and through his organization. In many ways, the relationship capital–building opportunity in this example is really with George Fraser.

George knows his clients. He is willing to back his clients. He vouches for them, which means he makes sure that the people he is talking about aren't flakes. He is the one who ensures that his company's networking sessions don't end up being mere networking events where people trade, then throw away, business cards.

I used to go to networking receptions and events early in my career, but at the time I was pretty much an "empty shirt," someone who looked the part but lacked the real substance to execute. I am not digging on me here; I am just making a factual point. I looked great, I said all the right things, but I was just selling, and selling does not build relationship capital.

I had business cards, I was dressed for success, and my cards had the number of a telephone answering service that served as my "office," but I had virtually no clients for my fledgling company. And so, I trundled off to networking receptions once or twice a week. Every week. And other than collecting a lot of business cards that I later did nothing with, I really cannot recall one thing of real value I got out of them.

When you go to networking receptions, you are often—please excuse my bluntness here—meeting other broke people. You are meeting other people who want the same thing that you do: to make the sell, any sell. Frankly, sometimes I just went for the free happy hour food, as I didn't have a budget for food or apartment rent when I first started in business. Everything was a hustle in those early years.

So, you have broke people trying to sell something to other broke people, something that oftentimes neither party wants, by the way. Do you think these broke people can help you get a good job, or make a substantial investment in your company? Probably not.

The people who can do those things don't go to networking receptions. They are at their offices, in their homes, or on planes somewhere, actually moving the agendas that they are already running. The folks you actually want to meet are running things, and they have no time (or interest) in attending random social events with random real value. They have better things to do.

Networking is basically only about the one doing the networking and what that person has to sell. It is a taker's activity and it is highly, highly transactional.

Relationship building is a giver's activity. It is about what you have to give, and it understands that real relationships are nurtured over time. Relationship building is a two-way street, with mutual benefit for both individuals.

Let me stop here to explain the difference between good selfishness and bad selfishness, because there is a direct correlation here with building relationship capital and networking.

Good selfishness is where I benefit you, and everyone else associated benefits more. Bad selfishness is where I benefit, but you and everyone else associated pay a price for it. One adds to society and our world, and the other just takes, depletes.

Raising your children is an example of good selfishness.

Running an ethical nonprofit organization is good selfishness.

Running for public office as a public servant (about *we*) and not just a being a politician (about *me*) is good selfishness.

Building and running a successful business that employs

people and provides a valuable product or service to society is good selfishness.

Building and running a day care service, or as in the case of my mother when I was growing up a nursery business, is good selfishness. I was my mother's first customer. She started the business as a creative way to spend more time with me and get paid doing it (smile).

A capitalist who builds a conglomerate and upon retiring directs the company to launch a major foundation focused on giving back to the communities that supported the company's growth and success is also good selfishness.

A drug dealer—whether in the underserved neighborhoods of South Central Los Angeles or the mansions of Bel Air— is an example of bad selfishness. No one is better off in this example except for the dealer. Everyone else comes out worse.

A thief is an example of bad selfishness. Someone who murders and steals for a living is an example of bad selfishness.

Those who use the cloak of public office or public service to line their own pockets are examples of bad selfishness.

Those who have been given the gift of the care of children, whether their own or others', and abuse this sacred right are probably the most egregious example of bad selfishness.

Building relationship capital, here or anywhere else around the world, is indeed good selfishness.

With networking, you don't even have to know someone. With relationship capital, you actually have to care.

Soon after founding Operation HOPE in 1992, I realized that I could not run the organization on hopes, dreams, goodwill, volunteers, and even my own money alone. I needed outside partners and supporters to help, but for two years almost no one would write a check to back my new organization other than me. Initially, this made sense, because if I didn't believe in HOPE enough to back it with my own money and sweat equity, then why should anyone else?

I remember driving clear out to Lancaster, California, almost two hours away, to meet with the CEO of a small community bank and ask him for a $1,000 investment in HOPE. After a couple of telephone conversations and a couple of visits, he did have the bank write the check for $1,000. In 1996, this was a big deal to me. My entire budget that year was something on the order of $61,000, most of which came from a government grant for small businesses. (It is worth noting that outgoing Los Angeles Mayor Tom Bradley [a black Democrat] had gone out of his way to arrange this modest but important SBA 7[j] grant for me and HOPE with outgoing President George W. Bush [a white Republican]. Operation HOPE was literally born in an environment of those with so-called differences finding pathways forward and common ground to work together. And now you know better why I am multiracial and bipartisan in my approach to life.)

The gentleman banker was Jack Seefus, then CEO of Antelope Valley Bank. In the course of our conversations I had become comfortable speaking informally to Jack, and so I gave him a hard time (after I got the $1,000 check, of course) about him being a CEO with nothing on his desk but a copy of the *Wall Street Journal.* I remember what he told me like it was yesterday.

"John, obviously, you have no idea what a CEO does every day. It is not my job to do home appraisals for values. I have hired home appraisers to do that. It is not my job to do credit underwriting for borrower applications. I have hired qualified people to do that. It is not my job to collect deposits or even manage the branch you are sitting in, John. I have hired qualified, wonderful people to do that. It is not my job to audit the books. I have a bunch of people who do that.

"John, it is my job to sit here with a clear head, to read the *Wall Street Journal* every day, and to chart the course forward for this organization, manage our risk, and to find new opportunities for the future. That's my job. And, by the way, that is why you are sitting here in front of me. You are my and our opportunity today."

I will never forget that. Lesson learned. And I read the *Wall Street Journal* now, religiously, these days from my iPad.

How a Relationship Saved Operation HOPE

My first real banker—meaning the first person who really backed me—was a gentleman by the name of William Hanna. I met William sometime after the Rodney King riots of 1992 when I was twenty-six years old and he ran a small community bank called Cedars Bank. William wanted to help the community, and I wanted to give him an intelligent way to do just that.

In those early years, we received only a modest amount of private-sector support for our work, and so I was forced to take a larger government grant to keep HOPE alive. But then, when the government shut down in 1994, I quickly discovered how thin the ice was underneath me. Very thin.

The federal government shut down and stopped issuing reimbursement payments, which meant we could not meet payroll. I called William because I knew he had the right spirit.

He wanted to be helpful, but he was a cautious type. He had seen far too many slick, fast-talking people come through his door with a dream to sell—using his wallet.

For two years, William had done little but sit and listen to me, but this was fine because I had a lot to say. He had taken my calls. He had met with me. He had even made a modest financial contribution to HOPE and had some of his team lend volunteer support to our effort. But none of this was consequential, really—to him or to me.

What I did not know was that he had been putting me through my paces, so to speak. He had been checking me out all this time. In many ways, he was underwriting me like I was a credit, like I was "capital." We were also building a real relationship based on trust. This relationship turned into a genuine friendship that sustains until this day.

I was in a bad way: HOPE's bank account was tapped, and I could not break another personal certificate of deposit to keep HOPE alive at that point. I had done all that I could to keep HOPE afloat. I needed outside assistance. And so, I called the man who for two years did mostly nothing but listen.

He answered the phone, and I said this: "William, the government has shut down, and I cannot get the reimbursements I need to pay my people. I am an honest man with an authentic calling, vision, and work. I need a short-term line of credit of $25,000 to pay my people, but all I have as collateral is my good name and my word." (My credit score back then was not the greatest, as I recall.)

I waited for the answer, and after what had to have been the longest minute of total silence in history, he said, "John, I will do this, and I will give you a year to pay me back. But you

MUST pay the bank back. This is my signature backing your dream here."

I gave William my word, and with this loan HOPE had a lifeline that has sustained it to this day.

Here is what I know now: William hung up that telephone and walked over to his chief financial officer, explaining the situation and circumstances to her. William told me years later that she said flatly, "No way should you do this, William. The bank cannot back this. It will not work. He will *not* pay you back. He is a nice young man but . . ."

But William quietly shut her down, saying that he was going to do this on his signature at the bank alone. And he told her, "You will see . . ."

I paid the full $25,000 back—in six months, not the twelve that the banker had given me. I had a point to make to him and his people and something to prove to myself. Years later, his CFO apologized to me for not believing in me for no good reason. But there was a good reason: she and I did not have a relationship, and I was outside of her circle of influence. It made perfect sense to me, and I didn't hold a thing against her.

My first banker started me out by entrusting me with a $25,000 credit line that even his own underwriters told him not to do. Less than a decade later, this same bank extended to me and HOPE a record $1 million line of credit, this time with the backing of the entire bank's credit underwriting staff. This loan even had several participants from other reputable banks (like Union and Wells Fargo Bank) who were willing to fund and share the risk with Cedars Bank.

I ended up with pure substance, but it began with a relationship.

It began with belief.

It began in that one bank office branch in Lancaster, California, with me getting one of my first notes on the Memo: relationships are investments.

The Best $100 I Ever Spent

For me, nothing is more important than my integrity and my name (collectively referred to as my brand). This is my real capital. Yes, I have some money, but that is not what I choose to focus on now, nor did I when I was a young man.

My black and brown friends where I grew up in South Central Los Angeles and Compton, California, were all focused on "getting paid."

Later in life, during the time that I was coming up as a young businessman and later as an entrepreneur, my white friends were focused on "getting rich."

I was not really interested in either.

I knew at a very early age that I wanted to *build wealth*, which has more to do with a perspective or a take on life than a pure statement of financial net worth.

Money would come and money would go, but I knew that if I ever truly discovered myself that I would have a value proposition that I could use, leverage, and lean on for the rest of my life. I knew that my true wealth lived within me, not in my wallet, let alone in someone else's wallet.

When I was eighteen, I asked an early mentor and my employer at the time, Harvey Baskin, to join me for dinner. Harvey was a successful businessman, a former financier, and the owner of Geoffrey's Malibu Restaurant, where I worked first as a not-so-good busboy, then as a not-much-better waiter, and later as Harvey's personal assistant. Harvey's leg was broken, and I had to drive him in my white Audi with the front seat folded forward so he could rest his leg while he sat in the back seat. It all looked like a very bad outtake from the movie *Driving Miss Daisy*.

We finally made it from Malibu, where Harvey lived, to the restaurant near Venice, California (his expensive, upscale choice, mind you), and I spent the entire time just plying him for information.

"How did you do this, Harvey? How did you do that? How do I navigate this? How do I move through this obstacle?"

My questions were nonstop and endless. But Harvey was patient with me, answering each and every one as best he could. Harvey finally did get frustrated with me, but it was at the very end of the dinner, and it had nothing to do with the probing questions I was asking him.

You see, I was Harvey's personal assistant, and let's just say that Harvey was brilliant at both making money and keeping it. He didn't waste much on salaries, but I still didn't realize in the moment how fortunate and blessed I was.

The bill for dinner came, and it was about $100, a small fortune for me back then. That may have been what I spent on food for the entire month at that age. Anyway, the bill came, and when I saw the amount, I asked, incredulously, "Harvey, you don't expect me to pay for this on the meager salary that you pay me, do you?"

Harvey's response was classic, bearing wisdom I hold with me as if it happened yesterday.

Harvey looked me straight in the eye and said, coolly, "John, you have to decide whether you want to pick my brain or my pockets. One lasts longer . . ."

And so, I paid the bill without another word, except thank you. Harvey had given me the priceless gifts of his wisdom, knowledge, and, most of all, his time—and I had initially "thanked" him with a crude attack on his wallet.

I decided that day what my priorities would be going forward: I was committed to building a wealth mentality, irrespective of what it cost me in the short term. I thought of it as investing in myself, in my own relationship capital. With the goal of transformational life change—at scale—I was going to get the Memo.

Don't Just Get a Job— Be Entrepreneurial

I don't like it when people refer to me first and foremost as an author, or a philanthropist, or a community leader, or an adviser to governments, or even a thought leader, as much high regard as that involves.

I am and always have been, first and foremost, an entrepreneur.

This is the attitude that has allowed me to survive, that has sustained my life, and, most of all, that has given me the continual edge on everyone trying to take my seat at the table of opportunity. It is my advantage when all the world is changing and closing in around me.

What everyone needs today—especially anyone looking to leave the Invisible Class—is to be entrepreneurial. It is a crucial survival skill in the twenty-first century when the only thing that is certain is change.

It really does not matter whether you want to be an entrepreneur. Regardless of what you do in life, you can benefit from thinking the way entrepreneurs think, from the way they approach life, solve problems, and even how they see problems. From the way they approach challenges and overcome things. From their optimism about everything.

It does not matter whether you are running a small bakery, or your household budget, or a government agency, whether you are managing a manufacturing plant or a Walmart shift. An entrepreneurial mind-set is precisely what you need in order to win in the twenty-first century.

The World, According to an Entrepreneur

Here are some of the ways that I as an entrepreneur see the world:

Success is going from failure to failure without loss of enthusiasm.

Most people believe that success is some grand, endless shopping spree. That is actually the perfect way to go broke. Most entrepreneurs are so busy chasing the dream and building out ideas for their lives that they have little time for much else (which is also a problem, but one for another day).

Real success is more about managing failure and disappointment without having it crush your spirit than it is about managing success (there is nothing very difficult about going on long vacations and enjoying the fruits of your labor).

As I quoted my friend Fred Smith, former president of

Operation HOPE, in my book *Love Leadership*, "Success is all about managing pain, the pain we create for ourselves, and the pain visited upon us by others."

I agree with Fred wholeheartedly. If you cannot successfully manage pain, then you cannot live a successful, sustained life.

Rainbows come only after storms. You cannot have a rainbow without a storm first.

Managing pain in a mature way gives one perspective on life. You understand that pain is not some penalty that God is visiting upon you. No one is punishing you. The universe is not targeting you. It is just simply a part of life—the storm before the rainbow.

When you have an entrepreneur's perspective, you wake up every day assuming that there are going to be problems and disappointments. You assume that you are going to get knocked down. You assume that those you love, and who say they love you, may end up kicking you when you are down. And that those who see you as a threat will undermine you, even when undermining them or anyone else was the last thing on your mind. An entrepreneur's mind-set teaches you—no, trains you—to do something that will not feel totally natural in these situations.

Your mind may suggest fear, and, thereafter, flight. But if you have an entrepreneur's mind-set it will almost instinctively instruct your *spirit* to get back up and to keep fighting. It does not instruct your body to do anything. It doesn't instruct your emotions to do anything. It instructs your spirit to double down with internal strength—your inner capital.

An entrepreneur's mind-set helps you to see a silver lining

in each and every situation presented to you. Think about it this way: even a knockdown (or a knockout) has the benefit of waking you up to ways to do things better the next time.

I take "no" for vitamins.

My friend Sally Mackin of the Woodlawn Foundation told me this, and I never forgot it: "I take 'no' for vitamins."

It does not matter what you tell me or say to me or how many times you tell me NO, I am still going to achieve my dreams! This was precisely my mind-set after my experience with homelessness at age eighteen.

I was homeless for six months due to believing too much of my own press, for wrongly being focused on "busyness" instead of real business. But I learned my lesson and got my head straight. I also became immune to failure after that. It just didn't bother me anymore.

I mean, what are you going to tell me when I walk in your door? You are going to tell me "no"? Well, I had "no" when I walked in the door. You cannot fall from the floor.

I decided I was good. I decided that I was enough. I would start where I stand. And then, I would stand taller.

It's hard to hit a moving target.

Fear is a punk. It is lazy, and it sits in the pits of the stomachs of those who allow it to immobilize them and their lives. It takes over people who become like deer caught between head-lights. They cannot move. But fear is useless against a believer. Or as I wrote in *Love Leadership*, "Courage is nothing more than your faith reaching through your fear, displaying itself as action in your life."

My approach is simple: Fear is lazy, and I am not. I am not lazy. I work. Hard. All the time. I keep moving, and it is hard to hit a moving target. So keep it moving.

Persistence and resilience are more powerful than pedigree and raw intelligence.

President Calvin Coolidge once famously said, "Press on: Nothing in this world can take the place of persistence. Talent will not; nothing is more common than unsuccessful men with talent. Genius will not; unrewarded genius is almost a proverb. Education will not; the world is full of educated derelicts. Persistence and determination alone are omnipotent" ("Those Persistent Coolidge Scholars," Kai's Coolidge Blog, June 14, 2012).

I have honorary doctorate degrees from colleges and special degrees and certificates from major universities, and I regularly do college commencement addresses at graduation, but the reality is that I have a GED high school degree. Comedian Chris Rock calls it a "Good Enough Diploma."

That said, my level of hustle is well known. As is my persistence. I will outwork you, outrun you, and outmaneuver you. I will wear you down on merit. Put me in a room filled with MBAs and PhDs, and I will run circles around them—not necessarily because I am smarter but because my level of persistence, resilience, and hustle is on an entirely different (higher) level.

What is your level of resilience and hustle? How persistent are you? Do you just throw your hands up at the first sign of injustice, of bias, of discrimination? Well, if that's the case, you will be dealing with nonachievement for the rest of your life, as the three things life will guarantee you are death, taxes, and unfair challenges.

Get over it, or get run over by it.

Life is 10 percent about what life does to you and 90 percent about how you respond to it.

People of the Invisible Class: you have to stop focusing on how you are treated and whether it is fair or right.

Assume that you will be treated unfairly.

Assume that life will be mostly unfair.

Assume that others won't do what is right.

Now what? I tell you what: Now, you change the game. You flip the script. You *decide* that while you cannot control what others do, you can absolutely control your *response* to those things. Life is 10 percent what life does to you and 90 percent how you choose to respond to life.

What is your response going to be?

Take your power back. Know that any reaction will be emotional and any decision made emotionally will be the wrong one. When you respond from the neck up, you take back your personal power over your own life. You regain control.

How full is your glass?

How you see the world absolutely determines your place in it and your ability to either move through your problems, get out of them, or remain trapped.

And here is a very simple truth: If you see the glass of life as half empty, then you are in a world of trouble. You are negative. You lack faith. This world will eat your lunch.

But if you see the world as a glass half full, well, then you are in luck. You are an optimist. You have belief. You have hope. As a result, you see ways through and out of problems. You are a problem solver. You will own this world.

An entrepreneur works eighteen hours a day to keep from getting a real job.

Entrepreneurs will work for free because they figured out what they were good at, and, more so, they found something they would do for free because they loved it. They love what they do. And for this reason alone, an entrepreneur or someone who is entrepreneurial has an advantage over the rest of the world.

Someone who is entrepreneurial will get up earlier, stay up later, think more intently, be more focused, behave more creatively, live more intelligently, and reimagine everything. Entrepreneurs love what they do so much they are willing to work for free if it means they don't have to get a traditional job. They want a purpose in and for their lives and not just a gig or a job to show up to.

What is your passion? Whatever that may be—whatever that passion is—it will be aided by the adoption of an entrepreneurial mind-set.

Get a job—or create one.

I have always said if you cannot get a job, then create one.

Those in the engrained power structure in any city or state always get the big jobs in the office towers. All the big jobs with existing benefits go to those within the power structure and those who know those within the power structure. In other words, people in the Invisible Class are left hanging.

So, what do you do if you can't get a job? You create one, just like the immigrants who came to America in the twentieth century in search of a better life.

From Ireland, Italy, Poland, and so many other parts of Western and Eastern Europe, these immigrants didn't know anyone. They had no power, no power structure, no power circles.

They were poor people who for the most part knew other poor people. But they also came looking for the American Dream with confidence and a measure of self-esteem (otherwise they would not have reached America's shores).

And so they created their own opportunities. They could not find jobs worth having, so they had no choice but to create their own jobs. And so, they hustled. They sold things. They made things. They traded things. They innovated; they made new things. They were entrepreneurs.

This wave of immigrants of the early twentieth century almost single-handedly seeded an entire generation of economic growth and jobs in America. They grew from nothing into something. They took an idea and turned it into a small business, and later grew that small business into a big one. In later periods, immigrants came from parts of Africa, Asia, and Latin America, and they responded to the same office tower challenge in the same way as those who came before them. And now, these immigrants from all over the world are the ones driving and powering the largest economy on the planet.

Drug Dealers Are (Illegal) Entrepreneurs

Speaking of creating jobs, at a recent Clinton Global Initiative America (CGI America) meeting, I spoke about my vision for the rewinning of America, and I gave the example of an inner-city drug dealer.

As we were talking about the power of the American idea, small business, entrepreneurship, and the thing we all need now—job creation—the simple question I posed to the audience of more than a thousand leaders was, "What do you think a drug dealer is, if not an illegal, unethical entrepreneur?"

The whole idea of drug dealers, and the gangs I grew up around in Compton, California, and South Central Los Angeles, actually turns my stomach. George, my-best-friend-from-childhood George, was killed while hanging out with the neighborhood drug-dealing thug. I believe drug dealing is both immoral and unethical, and there is a special place in hell reserved for anyone who sells death to their own people, in their own community, and in our schools.

That said, if someone is a "successful" drug dealer, the one thing that person is *not* is dumb.

These drug dealers understand import, export, finance, marketing, wholesale, retail, customer service, markup, up-selling, geography, territory, and of course security. They understand how to take an idea and, with very few natural resources available to them, make it real (maybe a bit too real) in people's lives.

In doing all of this—and yes again, it is unethical and illegal to its core—they do actually succeed in creating jobs for themselves and several others around them.

Of course, none of this is sustainable. There are no retired drug dealers. Their long-term options are prison, parole, or death. And given that they aren't paying their fair share of taxes on their ill-gotten gains to the Internal Revenue Service, their "careers" won't even *continue* for very long. Remember that the federal government did not finally convict gangster Al Capone for his long history of murder and mayhem but for tax evasion. The government *will* finally get you, one way or the other. I would rather simply pay my taxes (smile).

So why do so many of our low-wealth kids today want to be drug dealers, pop or rap stars, and professional athletes? It's a generalization that sadly happens to also be true. The answer is simple.

They want success just like you and I do, but where they live they are unfortunately modeling themselves on what they see. We need to give them something different to see.

At their core, the drug dealers and gang organizers in the inner-city neighborhoods of my childhood were brilliant organizers, strategists, and enterprise builders. They were natural hustlers and entrepreneurs. I heard of one particularly talented drug dealer who even issued corporate paychecks, complete with withholdings, to his "employees."

But, unlike myself, these young entrepreneurs-in-the-making had *horrible* role models, even worse home family environments, and ultimately a corrupt and unsustainable business model built on what I call "bad capitalism."

I was fortunate to grow up in a stable, albeit financially struggling, household, where my mother told me she loved me every day of my life, and my dad was a small business owner. My success path had been placed right in front of me. All I had to do was follow the path and not screw up. Most of my friends had it much worse.

Now, as I look for real and sustainable solutions to the poverty and lack of opportunity I see every day in my work at Operation HOPE, in our inner-city and rural communities across America, I am slowly coming to a strange conclusion.

These individuals, who are single-handedly destroying the very communities and the strong family structures that I am desperately trying to save, could also potentially help save it.

In order to be a successful entrepreneur, you have to be a contrarian, an out-of-the-box thinker (and doer), someone who takes risks, who is persistent and innovative, super hardworking, and someone who has a vision for themselves—the same traits you find in drug dealers and gang organizers.

As a nation, we are literally locking up (for nonviolent offenses) and tossing aside the 20 percent of society—young people with hustle and natural entrepreneurial energy—with the very same character traits that are required to raise up poor communities, create new jobs and markets, and grow local GDP.

What's often left over in underserved communities after we lock these young men and women up are the elderly and the infirm, the too-young-to-know-better, broken families, and traditional nine-to-five job seekers. Respectfully speaking, this is not exactly a prescription for economic growth and a stable tax base.

According to Malcolm Gladwell's book *The Tipping Point*, it takes only 5 percent of role models to stabilize any community.

Not 80 percent or 50 percent of models or 25 percent or even 10 percent. Just 5 percent. That's completely doable.

What would have happened if all the otherwise brilliant young people who wanted to become drug dealers, rap stars, and athletes (because these are the symbols of success that they see in their communities) had proper business role models or business internships growing up?

Maybe it would have changed everything. It did for me.

Embracing the Gig Economy

An entrepreneurial mind-set is crucial for everyone, but frankly not everyone is built to be an entrepreneur. That makes perfect sense, as entrepreneurs who build things also need committed groups of employees who can be collaborative builders of things.

The beauty of this new world we live in is that it is easy to be even a part-time entrepreneur on your own terms and start generating true wealth. That is what the gig economy is all about. It is a huge part of all the change and transformation going on, and you can make it work for you.

What does employment look like in this new world of ours? I can tell you what it is not: it is not a career at one company for twenty-five years. In fact, sometimes it barely even resembles traditional nine-to-five employment.

The gig economy is a labor market characterized by short-term contracts or freelance work as opposed to permanent jobs. Getting in on the gig economy can help you create your own economy. You are creating your own wealth, making your own choices, and, as a result, opening your eyes to the real possibilities and opportunities in the world.

Many of these short-term jobs and opportunities will not last, but a few of these jobs will turn into new occupations and even careers. And a few of these new small companies will become our traditional big companies of the future.

Uber and Lyft car services are excellent examples of gig economies.

I know countless Uber drivers who are not only making a decent living, they are also building wealth.

One Uber driver in Denver left a six-figure job at a major bank to create more freedom and choice and a better lifestyle for himself. A couple of years later, he had several cars under his Uber contract, was doing $1 million in revenue a year, and—of great importance to him—was creating jobs, choice, and more freedom for those he cared about in his local community.

Another Uber driver in Washington, DC, started out as the doorman at the Park Hyatt Hotel. He learned from the hotel guests how inefficient the taxi services were in the area as well as how—if given the chance—he could do better by them. And so, he did. He is now one of the top Uber drivers in the city.

And then you have gig economy jobs that actually feel like traditional-economy company opportunities. For instance, companies like Primerica Life Insurance Company allow you to be trained and certified in the insurance field, to receive an official franchise from a reputable company, and to start your own business building a sustainable income stream and, hopefully, a future foundation of financial wealth, all for a $100 investment. (*Disclaimer*: Primerica is a partner with Operation HOPE.)

Dermalogica, another partner with Operation HOPE, is steeped in the personal care, beauty, and wellness industry, which is not going away anytime soon. In fact, it is one of the fastest-growing and most sustainable industries in the world, and Dermalogica provides a wonderful, game-changing business ownership opportunity for entrepreneurial women who want to be a part of it. While automation is on the rise in many fields and will replace many job titles over the next couple of decades, no computer or robot is going to be giving you or me a facial anytime in the near (or far) future.

Dermalogica was started by my friend Jane Wurwand, who came to the United States with a little money, lots of moxie, a passion to become a change agent, and a marketable skill in skin care. Within a year, she and her mate started a business teaching others how to enter the skin care field. Today, Dermalogica benefits from both ends of the sales cycle: product development and sales, and skin therapist training. With more than 100,000 trained and certified skin therapists in the field today, around the world and on every continent, Dermalogica is one of the largest producers of trained skin care professionals in the world.

Personal campers, powerboats, and condos for rent are all examples of a gig economy.

Airbnb allows families and individuals to enhance their incomes while paying for a portion of their living expenses on their primary residences, or for the mortgages on their vacation homes. I have seen people rent their home, a room in their home, a shared room, or a camper in their driveway; there is even one person I know of in the Buckhead area of Atlanta who rented his finely crafted treehouse!

For the better part of three decades, I would see a camper driving on the freeway or a camper parked in the driveway of a home in the city, and I would think that this vehicle was at most a once-a-month-excursion recreation vehicle. I assumed that such a recreational vehicle was akin to a treadmill purchased and set up in your bedroom: once a fantastic dream, later converted into an expensive, useless clothes hook. But I was wrong.

One day I decided to take my family out to a racetrack where I planned to drive my Ford Shelby GT350R track car for the weekend outside of Atlanta. That said, I did not want my mother and family to freeze in the cool Georgia winter. And so, I decided to see if I could find a recreational vehicle with sleeping facilities for rent in Georgia. My computer exploded with possibilities.

I was shocked to learn that there were countless companies, including RVshare, Atlanta RV, and Cruise America, that did nothing but represent and rent these campers on freeways and campers in driveways while they were not in use by their owners. I paid a small fortune to rent one of these campers for that long weekend, so it is not hard to imagine that many owners might be able to pay for the cost of their vehicle over a short time simply through occasional yet consistent rental income from people like me. Brilliant. And this elegant little business model has now been applied to rental speed boats, houseboats, condos, and who knows what else?

Virtual assistants (VAs) are smart and capable people who generally work from home and on their own schedule. They work with clients that have specific needs—from administration to scheduling to project management. They are paid a good living wage, and they work under contract, meaning they or their clients can change the arrangement when they like. I know it works because I used VAs for me and other members of my senior leadership team at Operation HOPE over a period of a couple of years.

Grubhub, DoorDash, UberEATS, and Yelp Eat24 are even more examples of a gig economy. These food-delivery services are innovative solution makers for an increasingly busy, changing, and specialized, service-hungry world. They are also innovators that cut in on the traditional delivery model by doing things that had not previously been done—for example, creating centralized hubs where hungry people can search for, order, and pay for all different kinds of food in one place through the Internet—and, evidently, in a way that many people wanted. In so doing, they helped to create economic energy and expanded opportunity for restaurants and food-delivery service providers. More GDP. More gigs.

I heard of TaskRabbit through a close member of my family. When I met the representative they sent, a supersharp young man named Trevor Travers, it confirmed for me that there were hidden talent jewels in every corner of every city. Trevor soon stopped working for TaskRabbit and began working for me at Operation HOPE. He now works at HOPE while also earning extra money doing gig work with me in other areas, including special projects around my motorsports passion. Soon after, Trevor's friend David Triplet, who is equally skilled and super smart, joined the team. Together, they are now the core of my information technology (IT) team in Atlanta. Young, hungry for knowledge, and all "gigged up."

Etsy is essentially a virtual part-time store for innovators, entrepreneurs, and small business owners who don't have the capacity to do what Etsy does on their own. It is an online marketplace, a central portal for customers and providers alike, a sophisticated yet approachable marketer of specialized goods, a special place for innovators, and a trusted source for those who desire something unique.

These and other examples of gig economies are practical solutions to an economy that has fractured and torn in real time (as first observed by the mobile notary Eric McLean in my last book, *How the Poor Can Save Capitalism*). They are practical examples of how to get ahead in an economy that has shed jobs and entire sectors from the Industrial Revolution of the twentieth century and is busy mapping the demise of another 30 percent of jobs and sectors in the twenty-first century.

But as I have written in other parts of this book, new jobs are always being created, and entire new global industries—and new sectors—are emerging in their place. We are talking trillions of dollars of future GDP. And with a global economy at approximately $75 trillion today and a future global economy estimated to be more than $200 trillion, the only real questions are: Who will get their share of the remaining $125 trillion? And how can you make sure that it's you?

The answer? You make sure it's you by being entrepreneurial.

Here's a line, based on the Memo, for you to memorize: There has never been a global leader who was not an economic leader first.

Sometimes gifts and opportunities for the future feel like pain today. But that does not mean that they are not precisely that: opportunities for YOUR future.

Don't just get a job or just work at a job. Be entrepreneurial.

Be resilient. Hustle. Take "no" for vitamins. Always be on the lookout for opportunities to create your own economy. Understand that rainbows only follow storms, that you cannot have a rainbow without a storm first. It's not only good theory (and a nice story) but hard science and physics, too. It is part of getting the Memo.

Spiritual Capital Is the Start of True Wealth—Own Your Power

We are not human beings having a spiritual experience.
We are spiritual beings having a human experience.
PIERRE TEILHARD DE CHARDIN

L ife is all about energy. Think about everything that is important to you and in your life. I'm talking about love, charity, compassion, faith, belief, vulnerability, joy, confidence, self-esteem, empathy, sympathy, and countless other feelings of the heart.

But what do most people obsess about? Things. Homes, boats, cars, jewelry, clothes, and other things that blow away with the winds of time.

And this is precisely why most people are, well, miserable. Most people are looking for love in all the wrong places. In things.

If you want to get rich, then fine, focus your energy on things.

But if you want to gain wealth, true wealth, then learn to think differently, which I first talked about in Rule 2. Ambassador Andrew Young told me, "Real wealth comes from how you think, and not what you obsess about. Real wealth is about a certain view of the world. A perspective. A certain view of *yourself.*"

There is a difference between being broke and being poor. Being broke is a temporary economic condition, but being poor is a disabling frame of mind, a depressed condition of the spirit, a broken view of oneself.

True poverty has little to do with money.

To be clear, I am not talking here about sustenance poverty. Everyone deserves a roof over their head, food to eat, and the ability to take reasonable care of their health. Human dignity, basically. Everyone deserves this. But what next?

I am talking about building wealth beyond acquiring food, shelter, and basic health care needs.

I am talking now about a path to financial dignity—which begins with having spiritual wealth.

First of all, I am talking about self-esteem and confidence, which is half of the challenge in dealing with poverty and wealth. Because if you don't know who you are at 9 a.m., by dinnertime, someone else will tell you who you are.

I am talking about role models and your environment. Because if you hang around nine broke people, I can guarantee that you will be the tenth. Moreover, if you hang around nine wealth builders, you will also likely be the tenth.

The grandmother of my friend Dr. Regina Benjamin was an entrepreneur. She ran a business in town, and she was a landowner. Living in the rural South in the 1920s and 1930s, she was a role model, a transformational presence in her small town. Both Dr. Benjamin's grandmother and mother were strong female role models whose self-esteem, confidence, and spiritual wealth seeped into Regina's bones.

College was a forgone conclusion for Regina. It was not K–12 in her family—an education in her family meant K–college. Regina was also a joiner. She loved joining clubs. Well, the most popular club at Xavier University was for premed students, so she joined that club with confidence. Before she knew it, her environment was a network of type A achievers in the medical field.

In 2009, Regina became Dr. Regina Benjamin, our nation's eighteenth United States surgeon general.

Dr. Benjamin's family taught her the art and practice of hope, which leads me to my next point: I am talking about aspirations and opportunity. Aspiration is a code word for hope. And just as dollar bills are the currency of economic capital, hope is the currency of spiritual capital. Hope is the outward sign of spiritual wealth within.

Not only is the most dangerous person in the world a person with no hope, the opposite is also true: the most powerful person in the world is a person rooted in their own sense of hope.

Not in what people think about them.

Not in what their public image is.

Not in whether they are liked or not liked.

Not in whether they are admired, even, or whether they can play the game just right.

And certainly, not in what their net worth is or how many things they own or possess.

I am talking about a hope rooted in faith, based on love, and inspired by something larger and more important than oneself.

Hope is light in the world even when darkness is all around

us. Hope has its own "true north" even when everyone else is pointed in the opposite direction. Even when everyone else may disagree, hope lives on.

Only with hope can you become "reasonably comfortable" in your own skin—and the most powerful asset you can have in your life is to be reasonably comfortable in your own skin. For me, it has been the essence of my spiritual power, and it has created my spiritual wealth. It is my personal secret sauce.

You cannot have hope, particularly when the world seems to be working against you, without being reasonably comfortable in your own skin.

Dr. Cecil "Chip" Murray once told me, "It's not what people call you, it is what you answer to that is most important," and to "never, ever, answer out of your name." That's what you do if you are reasonably comfortable in your own skin. If you have built spiritual capital. If your path is fueled by hope.

Hope reminds us that badness is failed goodness. It reminds us that darkness has no definition without light.

Even that punk Lucifer from the Bible was once an angel, which means that even God Almighty gives the devil permission to exist. That is how powerful hope is—it is a first cousin of the One That Is.

Human evil does not exist outside of yourself, nor does spiritual goodness. All of it actually rests inside of yourself. And both sides are fighting for domination of your day. Every. Single. Day.

So the questions become: Who is winning, and what does winning take? Better still, do we need to fundamentally rethink what winning looks like?

Real Power Allows Everyone to Win

My best friend, Rod McGrew, once told me, "When you really have the power, you don't need to use it." He is right. But you won't have the power, or even truly understand it, if you can't get out of your own way.

Let's go back to the question of what "winning" looks like. The traditional view is that in order for me to win, you must in turn lose. But in Dr. King's, Andrew Young's, and Nelson Mandela's worldviews, the aperture opens wide enough to allow everyone to win. In fact, their worldviews pretty much require it.

Dr. King believed that a minority group could not win based on raw, brute strength. He had no military and no inventory of bombs and bullets, and so, his movement needed a different strategy to win, one in which the persecuted minority group took the moral high ground in every instance. His brilliant strategy was to wrap up the interests of the so-called enemy in the win for the oppressed minority group.

As a result, Dr. King was often the only black leader talking constructively to white America, at a time when the majority of black leaders were talking exclusively to Black America. In the latter example, it was far too easy to fall back on the unseen and unheard pain of the oppressed. The publicly expressed pain of the black community that came as a result often became the product itself or the "win." But in reality it was only emotional, short-term public therapy for a depressed and hurt people. These leaders won the battle, but never won any wars worth celebrating. There was no achievement for those represented beyond a "feel-good" acknowledgement of their pain.

My modern approach to solving our problems builds on the moral authority of Dr. King, the diplomacy of Andrew Young, a spirited dash of Malcolm X ("You've been took. You've been hoodwinked. Bamboozled . . ."), the gumption of Dr. Dorothy Height ("John, I like you because you are a dreamer with a shovel in your hands"), the broad-based engagement of President Abraham Lincoln, the sophistication of Frederick Douglass, and the disruptive innovation of Steve Jobs.

And here it is, in the words of Dr. Cecil "Chip" Murray: "Talk without being offensive. Listen without being defensive. And always, always leave even your adversary with their dignity. Because if you don't, they will spend the rest of their life working to make you miserable. It becomes personal."

When you can leave your adversaries with their dignity— which is possible only when you possess spiritual wealth (i.e., you know who you are, are reasonably comfortable in your own skin, and are acting out of hope and faith in your future)—the very next movement is simple achievement for the individual or group in question. Achievement.

Gaining spiritual wealth—and, therefore, true wealth—is about leveling the playing field and then sharing the field of advancement, not blowing up the field. But none of this is even remotely possible if you are angry or if payback or settling scores is the object of the game.

No one can afford today to be "angry for a living," least of all us members of the Invisible Class.

Real winners learn to step over mess, never in it. Real winners don't rearrange the deck chairs on the Titanic of their lives.

"The ship is sinking, and we are busy picking drapes!" cannot be our rallying cry.

True wealth is about taking your life back. Owning yourself from here on out.

Getting Out of Your Own Way

My friend Quincy Jones says that we are all "terminals for a higher power."

In fact, the entire purpose of life just might be about becoming transparent to God's will, about learning to get out of your own way. Truth be told, I spend my entire day trying to get out of my own way.

So, what is the problem? Ourselves. Me. You. Us.

I remember asking my friend the world-renowned philosopher Dr. Pekka Himanen, a cofounder of Global Dignity, what matters most in life. He gave me a different answer. He told me that the thing that matters most is what we are most afraid of: ourselves.

We are afraid of our true selves.

There are the public parts of us that we hold up to the world to view, for example, our Facebook profile pages and our Instagram feeds.

And then there are the private parts that we are on some level ashamed of or afraid to show the world for fear of being judged.

The first narrative—the public part of ourselves—is broadcast and shared with the world through something we call our personality. The word *personality* comes from the Latin root word *persona* or "to perform."

Our personality is the performance we put on for the world.

It is not necessarily fraudulent or dishonest, but it might just be a vehicle to keep everyone at a distance from our true, private selves. Call it self-preservation.

In the case of some, the public persona is a full-on replacement of the true self, because we believe it looks better. Sadly, this is the beginning of all bad things in our lives.

With our public self, we get to be perfect only twice: when we are born and when we meet someone for the first time. And so, we often "subcontract" our true selves to caricatures that we believe are more interesting than our realities. Touched-up social media photos all too often show a better side of us than what actually exists, and so we claim the better look as our own.

This is just about the opposite of being reasonably comfortable in our own skin.

Spiritual Poverty and Addiction

When we don't show up whole, comfortable, and present in our own lives, a bunch of behaviors begin to take up residence in our lives: drinking, drug taking, smoking, complaining, over-indulgence in sex, excessive shopping, oversleeping, uncontrolled social media posting, and a long list of other addictions. But none of this is really sustainable. None of this represents spiritual wealth.

Addictions are reactions to emotions we cannot handle. When we have not healed from the real pain in our lives and we have these addictions disguised as "happy time" busily taking up occupancy in our emotional lives, things start to get worse—fast.

When there is a hole in the bottom of the emotional cup of our lives, it does not matter how much you pour into it. The cup still has a hole. Every day, it takes more and more of the same thing to give us the same release. This is how people die: more and more of the wrong thing poured into their emotional cups. And long before the body dies, the spirit goes first.

Increasingly, what we are experiencing here in the United States and internationally is a crisis of spiritual poverty. A world that is full of fear and fading hope. A world of people—good people, God's children—who simply do not feel seen.

Hope is the antidote to fear. Regaining your sense of self is the antidote to spiritual poverty.

The first step is finding your Identity Project. I am convinced that the way to save the Invisible Class and all our young people who are at high risk of losing hope is to help them figure out their Identity Projects.

Once you know who you are, you start to believe in yourself and your future. You begin building spiritual capital. You refocus your attention on positivity and finding your way out of the lonely wilderness of depression and fear.

From your Identity Project—which you can think of as the beginning of a genuine embrace of your true inner self—you can then begin to figure out your purpose. What are you here to do, and how are you going to start doing it?

Dr. Martin Luther King Jr. once said, "If you don't know what you are willing to die for, then you are not fit to live."

Without hope, without purpose, there is no spiritual wealth. There is no true wealth.

Quieting the Mind Lets the Spirit Flow

Now that we have tapped into the real power within us—our spiritual power—let's deal with that mind of ours.

Most of us have given our mind way too much credit. Way too much power. We have promoted the mind beyond its pay grade. We have placed the mind in charge of our lives, and then we wonder why we feel like we are going crazy on a daily basis.

Why are we going crazy? Because the mind was never meant to be placed in charge of our lives. Remember, we are spiritual beings having a human experience, not the other way around.

My chief of staff, Rachael Doff, once asked a loved one, "Can you please give that other person inside of you—the one telling you all of this destructive, crazy, negative stuff—can you please give this other person inside of you a name and then tell them to go kiss-off?"

The spirit and the soul are the command centers for your life. Not your mind. You need to quiet your mind and then focus it.

But before you can quiet and focus your mind, you have to better understand the two sides of the mind. The left brain is the analytical side. This is where we do computation, research, and processing of data and facts. Hold on to this factoid for a moment while I speak about the right side of the brain. The right side of the brain is where creativity lives. It is where aspiration, hope, dreams, and all our wild ideas live.

Now here is something to think about: if your spirit is distressed, and your hope is under house arrest, then what is there for the right side of the brain to get excited about and to dream about?

Where is the positive energy mind food that triggers the firing of endorphins on the right side of the brain? Where are the endorphins that cause dream making and aspiration to fire in the mind? Where is the right-brain activity that then triggers the left side of your brain to work on a detailed and rational plan to execute your dreams?

Said a different way, if you are depressed and hopeless, you probably won't be making much positive use of your left brain, the analytical mind. And, worse, because of the emotional darkness taking up residence within, your decisions are likely to be emotional reactions rather than rational responses. Emotional, angry, maybe even dark.

The enemy of your progress has now got you right where they wanted you all along: off your game.

When you are depressed, you get something called "cognitive narrowing." In other words, when you are depressed, your IQ drops temporarily. (My exploration of the links between the cognitive sciences and modern poverty, spiritual wealth, hope, and finally behavioral economics—which are used by companies and organizations, both honorable and not so honorable, to target all of us for offerings we might be susceptive to more often than not—was inspired by the work of author and thinker Milhaly Csikszentmihalyi in his book *Flow: The Psychology of Optimal Experience.*)

When the neurons are sparking in your brain and spirit, you enter into a state of "aspirational mind," where you gain "cognitive expansion," particularly on the right side of your brain where hope, aspiration, and dreams live. Through cognitive expansion you temporarily achieve an IQ increase.

In short, the spiritual wealth I speak about here will make you smarter, and over time more successful. Likewise, the increasing, persistent stranglehold of spiritual poverty, or a poverty mind-set, will decrease your mental energy, which will decrease your capacity for individual economic energy. And individual economic energy is the origin of what the world calls GDP.

Said plainly, a poverty state of mind, an increasing hopelessness and faithlessness, dooms you to a future of increasing economic despair.

It becomes a cycle like any other cycle feeding on itself, adding fuel to an already strained existence.

Picture this: A single head of household, working and commuting fourteen hours a day, with bad role models in a bad environment, a beaten-down sense of self-esteem, low confidence in himself and his skills, dashed dreams, and too much month at the end of his money.

Without the right mind-set and spirit, darkness will surely come.

Now add financial illiteracy to this toxic mix of generational economic lack, lower levels of education, a general sense of hopelessness, depression, and no self-confidence, and you have the perfect cocktail for the targeted, systematic societal abuse that is evident in almost every 500-credit-score neighborhood across America. Be the inhabitants black or white, urban or rural, the crisis is essentially the same.

And this is precisely why I believe that the mostly untold

story of the Freedman's Bank carries so much historical significance.

The Freedman's Savings Bank was created to teach former slaves about money and the free-enterprise system back in 1865. Today, there are a few billion people or more throughout the world who need to get the same Memo.

The top 10 percent of adults in the world hold 85 percent of the total wealth in the world, while the bottom 90 percent hold the remaining 15 percent of the world's total wealth. Now certainly, this first group got the Memo on money. But what about the rest of us?

That said, this is much more than a story about money. Money has a communicated energy of its own, and that energy—how and where it flows, where it sits and settles, who has it and who loses it—is also an understanding we must master. There is a whole new language that we must learn: the language of money.

Ultimately, this is a story about us surviving or thriving. About whether we just barely make it and accept that as enough for us, for our children, and for our community, or whether we work together for a shared aspiration: a better life for us all.

While it is true that we are all God's children, and thus all of our challenges and opportunities and potential are essentially the same, some of us (i.e., those in the Invisible Class) start from different places. This unlevel playing field must be called out and made plain. It must be acknowledged. It is an obvious, and in some cases, historic disadvantage for some. But it can also be a hidden strength.

You see, rainbows only follow storms. You cannot have a

rainbow without a storm first. And loss creates leaders, as I detailed in my book *Love Leadership: The New Way to Lead in a Fear-Based World.*

I grew up in South Central Los Angeles and Compton, California, and this made me hustle *more.* I was not born into a family of higher education degree holders, and I got a GED degree out of high school. That said, I am a lifelong learner. My home office and my corporate office are both filled with books. My home office is, literally, a book library.

I was homeless for six months of my life at eighteen years of age. This no doubt made me stronger. Once I emerged on the other side from this humiliating experience, I was not only more resilient, I was more confident in myself. I was less concerned about what someone else thought about me, less concerned about my short-term image, hoisted and promoted by others, and much more concerned about my long-term, internal growth, chartered and navigated by me. I was curating a new me for the twenty-first century.

I realized that nothing much could kill the very thing I needed the most: my undying spirit.

This newfound understanding allowed me to redefine "success" in my life as "going from failure to failure without loss of enthusiasm."

It has allowed me to take "no" for vitamins to this very day. Every day.

I don't get worked up when a crisis comes. I tend to manage my emotions. I get calmer. More settled. I find my internal light in the midst of each and every crisis, and I sit down in it. In so doing, I become "enlightened." And this is where I find most of the answers to my problems. I never make a decision with my mind. My decisions are 100 percent intuitive, which requires a quieting, a sitting down, being present.

And this is why we must talk without being offensive, listen without being defensive, and leave even our adversaries with their dignity. Or else we will never get out of the mess we collectively find ourselves in.

Spiritual power does not need to exact revenge. It does not need to bludgeon an offender just because we can. Spiritual power is also about forgiveness—not because the other person deserves it, because often they do not. But because we do. We deserve to—and often need to—let it go.

Hating someone else hurts and destroys only the person doing the hating. There is no peace or quiet with hate. And it takes valuable time and energy away from your true pursuit: being present in your own curated and created life.

Creating Your Own Spiritual Wealth

There are three ways to live: coping (i.e., dealing with it), suicide (i.e., giving up), and healing (i.e., moving on). Most people are just coping. Suicide is not really an option. Healing is the only way forward. Gaining spiritual wealth is part of the healing process of this life.

Spiritual wealth is about becoming perfect in our imperfections. It is about finding that little light deep inside of yourself and sitting down there. Just sitting there and being enlightened. Embracing yourself. Being present in your own life.

To quote Eckhart Tolle from *The Power of Now:* "Yesterday is a memory, and does not exist. Tomorrow is the future, and has not happened. Neither exist. Neither are real, but most of us have one foot in yesterday, and one foot in tomorrow. Which is why we're not present in our own lives."

Most of us are obsessed and distracted by our unhealed past, or worse, we live in the future, thinking that when we move to a new city, get a new job, or marry a new beloved, all our problems will be solved.

Not only do these false narratives rob you of the only thing that *is*—this present moment—but they are also robbing you of precious time and valuable resources. Time that could be focused on and directed toward the only thing that should matter: Taking Your Life Back.

The moment when we realize this little jewel is the moment we begin to accumulate true spiritual wealth.

"Life is difficult."

This is the first line in Dr. Scott Peck's bestselling book *The Road Less Traveled*. If you can't get with this statement, then don't bother reading the rest of this groundbreaking book on becoming your true self.

What you see depends on where you sit. No one promises you a rose garden, and it is up to you whether you think that the rose bush has a few thorns or the thorn bush also includes a rose. It is your choice.

What are you choosing in your life?

What are you telling yourself?

Do you realize that "thoughts are things," to again quote my friend Rod McGrew?

Do you realize that you are changing the chemical makeup of your brain, and the energy in your body, based on how you see, feel, and interact with the world?

Are you ready to become the Knight of the Round Table in

your life? The lead protector for your family? The leader for your community?

Are you ready to take your life back?

These are the questions you must be prepared to answer before you can claim spiritual wealth.

It is the first step in introducing your own greatness, which will then allow you to pursue your dreams of economic liberation, whether they are owning a home, starting a small business, or becoming an entrepreneur.

Consider that nearly half of all employers require a credit check before they will hire you. When you get the Memo, you have the tools to raise your credit score to 700 (Operation HOPE can help, too), and in the process reclaim *you*. When your aspirations rise and your credit score rises, so does your well-being. So does your self-esteem. Your confidence. Your options in life.

At Operation HOPE, we teach you that if you can't get a job, you can create one. You can become your own self-employment project. But all of this takes spiritual fortitude. Spiritual wealth is the foundation.

CONCLUSION:
This Is Your Memo

The civil rights movement was waged and won in the streets, but the silver rights movement will be waged and won in the suites.

Civil rights was about race and the color line, but silver rights is about class and poverty. If you deal with class, you often get race for free. It is time for a new movement, and its color is green (as in the color of money).

But wealth—just like poverty—begins in the heart, the soul, and the mind before it ever ends up in your pockets.

We must remember that we are our first capital. We are the CEOs of our own lives.

We are investors *and* investments.

We are holders of relationship capital.

We are translators and transmitters of our dreams.

We must become lifetime learners.

We must never give up our childlike curiosity, our hope, and our joy.

We must accept that there is no one else just like us on this entire planet.

And then we must embrace this reality, acquiring self-esteem and confidence, absent of arrogance and unnecessary ego.

Ultimately, we must claim our own definitions of ourselves. We must own that most precious and invaluable asset—our self-determination.

But you cannot self-determine without first getting the Memo.

The Memo is all the important stuff in the world that no one bothered to tell you, yet alone to teach you, about how to make your inner capital—your mind-set, your relationships, your entrepreneurial skills, and, most of all, your spiritual wealth—work for you toward your economic liberation.

This is your Memo.

RESOURCES:
So You Got the Memo. Now What?

One of the first steps to economic independence is financial literacy. Here is a list of financial education resources to help you "know what you don't know" and to put what you know into action. And, of course, Operation HOPE is here to work with you every step of the way. Visit us online at www .operationhope.org.

Credit Cards and Credit Scores

Federally mandated free credit report:
www.annualcreditreport.com

FICO scores from all three credit bureaus (paid subscription):
www.myfico.com

Credit card reviews, ratings, and comparisons:
www.cardratings.com

Tools to create your own debt elimination plan:
powerpay.org/

Guidance on becoming debt-free:

www.wikihow.com/Get-Out-of-Debt

Guidance on choosing a credit card,
filing for bankruptcy, and repairing your credit:

www.operationhope.org/credit-guidance

Retirement

A starter retirement savings option from
the US Department of the Treasury:

www.myra.gov

Kiplinger Retirement savings calculator:

www.kiplinger.com/tool/retirement/T047-S001-retirement
-savings-calculator-how-much-money-do-i/index.php

AARP retirement planning calculator:

www.aarp.org/work/retirement-planning/
retirement_calculator.html

Banking Basics

A comprehensive financial education curriculum from
the US Federal Deposit Insurance Corporation:

www.fdic.gov/consumers/consumer/moneysmart

Financial education article portal:

www.finweb.com

Personal finance articles and advice:

www.kiplinger.com

Frequently asked questions about debit cards:

www.dfi.wa.gov/financial-education/information/
debit-cards-frequently-asked-questions

Understanding savings, credit, checking,
and retirement accounts:

www.operationhope.org/banking-basics

Home Ownership

Tools and resources for homebuyers:

www.consumerfinance.gov/owning-a-home

A guide to starting the home-buying process:

www.thebalance.com/buying-a-home-guide
-to-getting-started-1798294

Buying a home in ten steps:

money.cnn.com/pf/money-essentials-home-buying/index.html

Guidance on homeowner insurance policies:

money.cnn.com/pf/money-essentials-home
-insurance-policy/index.html

Tools to calculate mortgage payments, compare loan
offers, and analyze homeownership tax breaks:

www.mortgageloan.com/calculator

The basics of owning a home:

www.operationhope.org/home-ownership

Taxes

Choosing a tax preparer:

www.irs.gov/uac/points-to-keep-in-mind
-when-choosing-a-tax-preparer

Tax filing basics:

www.thebalance.com/tax-filing-basics-4073924

Taxes you have to pay:

money.cnn.com/pf/money-essentials-taxes/index.html

Understanding form W-2 and wage and tax statements:

www.thebalance.com/understanding-form
-w-2-wage-and-tax-statement-3193059

Requirements for the Earned Income Tax Credit:

www.irs.gov/credits-deductions/individuals/
earned-income-tax-credit

The ins and outs of tax preparation:

www.operationhope.org/taxes

Small-Business Entrepreneurship

How to decide if entrepreneurship is right for you:

guides.wsj.com/small-business/starting-a-business/
how-to-decide-if-entrepreneurship-is-right-for-you

Free online education for entrepreneurs:

www.scu.edu/mobi/business-courses

Deciding on the legal form your business should take:

www.inc.com/articles/2003/09/legal.html

How to form an LLC (limited liability company):

guides.wsj.com/small-business/
starting-a-business/how-to-start-an-llc

How to register a company name trademark:

guides.wsj.com/small-business/starting-a-business/
how-to-trademark-a-company-name

Reducing your small business tax bill:

www.inc.com/guides/reduce-smb-tax.html?nav=related

Guidance on starting your own business:

www.operationhope.org/small-business-entrepreneurship

INDEX

ABOUT THE AUTHOR

 **John Hope Bryant** is an American entrepreneur, author, philanthropist, and prominent thought leader on financial inclusion, economic empowerment, and financial dignity. Bryant is the founder, chairman, and chief executive officer of Operation HOPE, Inc.; chairman and chief executive officer of Bryant Group Ventures and The Promise Homes Company; and cofounder of Global Dignity. His work has been officially recognized by the last five US presidents, and he has served as an adviser to the previous three sitting US presidents. He is responsible for financial literacy becoming the policy of the US federal government. In January 2016, Bryant became the only private American citizen to inspire the renaming of a building on the White House campus when the US Treasury Annex Building was renamed the Freedman's Bank Building. The Freedman's Bank legacy has become the narrative of the work of Operation HOPE—to help all people become fully integrated into our nation's economy.

A member of the founding class of the Forum of Young Global Leaders, and founding member of Clinton Global Initiative, Bryant is a LinkedIn Influencer, contributor to the *Huffington Post* and *Black Enterprise*, and a member of the World Economic Forum's Expert Network. His Facebook Live "Silver Rights" series has received millions of views and serves as an engaging platform to foster essential discussion in the digital space around financial inclusion and social uplift. He has received hundreds of awards and citations for his work, including Oprah Winfrey's Use Your Life Award, and the John Sherman Award for Excellence in Financial Education from the US Treasury.

Bryant was named *American Banker* magazine's 2016 Innovator of the Year, and one of *Time* magazine's 50 Leaders for the Future in 1994. He is the author of *How the Poor Can Save Capitalism: Rebuilding the Path to the Middle Class* (Berrett-Koehler), and *Love Leadership: The New Way to Lead in a Fear-Based World* (Jossey-Bass).

ABOUT OPERATION HOPE

The mission of Operation HOPE, Inc. is silver rights empowerment, making free enterprise work for everyone. We accomplish this through our work on the ground as the nonprofit private banker for the working poor, the underserved, and the struggling middle class. We achieve our mission by being the best-in-class provider of financial literacy empowerment for youth, financial capability for communities, and ultimately, financial dignity for all.

Since its inception in 1992, HOPE has served more than 2.5 million individuals. HOPE has also directed more than $2.8 billion in private capital to America's low-wealth communities, maintains a growing army of twenty-two thousand HOPE Corps volunteers, and currently serves more than three hundred US cities, as well as Morocco, Saudi Arabia, South Africa, and the United Arab Emirates.

See more at www.operationhope.org.

Berrett–Koehler
Publishers

Berrett-Koehler is an independent publisher dedicated to an ambitious mission: *Connecting people and ideas to create a world that works for all.*

We believe that the solutions to the world's problems will come from all of us, working at all levels: in our organizations, in our society, and in our own lives. Our BK Business books help people make their organizations more humane, democratic, diverse, and effective (we don't think there's any contradiction there). Our BK Currents books offer pathways to creating a more just, equitable, and sustainable society. Our BK Life books help people create positive change in their lives and align their personal practices with their aspirations for a better world.

All of our books are designed to bring people seeking positive change together around the ideas that empower them to see and shape the world in a new way.

And we strive to practice what we preach. At the core of our approach is Stewardship, a deep sense of responsibility to administer the company for the benefit of all of our stakeholder groups including authors, customers, employees, investors, service providers, and the communities and environment around us. Everything we do is built around this and our other key values of quality, partnership, inclusion, and sustainability.

This is why we are both a B-Corporation and a California Benefit Corporation—a certification and a for-profit legal status that require us to adhere to the highest standards for corporate, social, and environmental performance.

We are grateful to our readers, authors, and other friends of the company who consider themselves to be part of the BK Community. We hope that you, too, will join us in our mission.

A BK Life Book

BK Life books help people clarify and align their values, aspirations, and actions. Whether you want to manage your time more effectively or uncover your true purpose, these books are designed to instigate infectious positive change that starts with you. Make your mark!

To find out more, visit **www.bkconnection.com**.

Berrett–Koehler
BK Publishers

Connecting people and ideas
to create a world that works for all

Dear Reader,

Thank you for picking up this book and joining our worldwide community
of Berrett-Koehler readers. We share ideas that bring positive change into
people's lives, organizations, and society.

To welcome you, we'd like to offer you a free e-book. You can pick from
among twelve of our bestselling books by entering the promotional code
BKP92E here: http://www.bkconnection.com/welcome.

When you claim your free e-book, we'll also send you a copy of our e-news-
letter, the *BK Communiqué*. Although you're free to unsubscribe, there are
many benefits to sticking around. In every issue of our newsletter you'll find

- A free e-book
- Tips from famous authors
- Discounts on spotlight titles
- Hilarious insider publishing news
- A chance to win a prize for answering a riddle

Best of all, our readers tell us, "Your newsletter is the only one I actually
read." So claim your gift today, and please stay in touch!

Sincerely,

Charlotte Ashlock
Steward of the BK Website

Questions? Comments? Contact me at bkcommunity@bkpub.com.

 MIX
Paper from
responsible sources
FSC® C011935
www.fsc.org

 Certified
Corporation
bcorporation.net